THE 7 RINGS

A JOURNEY TO A BALANCED LIFE OF PEACE, PASSION, AND PURPOSE

BRIAN WATSON

THE 7 RINGS

A JOURNEY TO A BALANCED LIFE OF PEACE, PASSION, AND PURPOSE

ISBN: 978-1-942306-87-0

Cover design & interior layout | Yvonne Parks | PearCreative.ca
Photos of Brian Watson taken by Molly Johnson | mollyjohnson-photography.com

DEDICATION

This book is dedicated to my father Bill Watson who passed away when I was a teenager, and to my dad Bob Lambrigger who recently passed before this book was printed. I was blessed to have two different fathers in my life. Although the loss of each was emotional and tragic, they will both be remembered with respect, admiration, and love.

TABLE OF CONTENTS

WHAT WILL YOU DO WITH YOUR LIFE TODAY?

"Success is liking yourself, liking what you do, and liking how you do it." | **Maya Angelou**

I've noticed an interesting paradox in the past few years. On one hand, media commentators, researchers, and historians tell us the American Dream is dead. Some even go so far as to say it has become a nightmare, a mirage of materialism promising the false hope of personal fulfillment to everyone when in reality it only delivers to a few privileged powerbrokers. Most of these naysayers claim our country has already peaked as a world leader and is now in decline.

When our country was founded, however, the United States served as a land of opportunity, an untamed wilderness offering a better life than the lingering social caste system of feudal European countries, such as

England and France, could provide. If people were willing to brave the voyage to America, risk facing its dangers and uncertainties, and work hard, then a better life potentially awaited them. The Declaration of Independence promised that "all men are created equal" with the right to "Life, Liberty and the pursuit of Happiness." Consequently, our great nation became the proverbial melting pot of various ethnicities and cultures, races and tribes. Even today in the 21st century, thousands of people enter the U.S. each year, and immigration—who and how many to allow into our country—remains a controversial issue.

Yet many people insist the American Dream has died somewhere over the course of the past two-hundred-plus years, that cultural cynicism has replaced the optimism upon which our country was built. But here's the paradox: if the American Dream is dead, then why do so many people still yearn to enter our borders any way possible as they seek a better, fuller, more exciting, and satisfying life? Why do so many people seem determined to chase success and keep their dreams alive?

WINNING IS EVERYTHING—OR IS IT?

Everyone wants to be a winner, a success, a person who makes the most of their God-given talents, abilities, and opportunities to improve their own life and the lives of others. Maybe this is human nature and not something unique to our country. But I believe growing up in a land where someone without a college education can become a self-made billionaire through their talent and hard work creates a special atmosphere, a sense of possibility that underdogs can slay the giant odds against them by sheer will and tenacity.

Simply put, people love winning. From the ball field to the battlefield, from a board game to the boardroom, winning seems to be an integral part of being human. In fact, our brains are genetically hardwired to pursue winning. Whether we're hunting wild animals to survive like our ancestors or chasing our next promotion on the corporate ladder or purchasing a raffle ticket, scientists tell us winning unlocks a flood of feel-good neurochemicals including dopamine, serotonin, and oxytocin. Winning clearly has the power to make us feel good.

In the United States, along with many other countries, we are conditioned to compete from birth, in everything from academics to athletics and every extracurricular activity imaginable. In fact, researchers tell us children today feel more pressure to win at an earlier age (www.nytimes.com/2013/02/10/magazine/why-can-some-kids-handle-pressure-while-others-fall-apart.html). This pressure to win continues as young adults jockey for awards, scholarships, and admission to the best universities. After earning degrees, they then begin the lifelong process of competing for jobs. In the tumultuous economy of the past few years, such competition has often determined the difference between financial success or bankruptcy.

Even our primary leisure activities focus on winning. Spectator sports such as football, baseball, basketball, soccer, and auto racing have become billion dollar industries, each with its own particular championship title of "world's best." With video games, players can challenge other players as well as imaginary adversaries in their quest to advance to the next level where the pursuit of the winning cycle begins again. On TV there is a flood of reality shows focused on competition in every category: singing, cooking, decorating, modeling, and even dating. Whether by achievement or popular vote, or a combination of both, participants strive to win at any cost.

RINGS AROUND YOUR CORE

Yes, everyone wants to win, to succeed—but what does that mean in each of our lives? And just as important as succeeding, doesn't it matter *how* you win? I'm convinced these two big questions are at the heart of what it means to be truly successful. Because chasing your American Dream is about more than having a better job, making more money, and buying more stuff. It's about creating a balanced life of fulfillment, getting up each morning with a passion to face your day and live out your divine purpose. It's about enjoying your family and the relationships around you, actively engaging in each other's lives, taking time to talk with people and better yet, to truly listen to them. It's about loving what you do and contributing to make the world a better place.

I've definitely not reached a level that's anywhere close to perfect, but I have learned how to live in synchronicity with the way I'm made and the life I've been given. While there's no magic formula or three easy steps, I believe seven areas of life require your attention, cultivation, and investment. I think of them as seven rings, sometimes overlapping and intersecting one another. More three-dimensional and dynamic than flat and static, these seven rings are not concentric like a bullseye or free-floating like bubbles. They are more like parts of an atom swirling around its nucleus or satellites orbiting a planet.

I've come to call them the "7 Rings of Life" and they're mostly based on various experiences and events in my own life, which have often been painful and challenging. The older and wiser I've become (at least, I hope I've become), the more clarity I have received regarding the positioning of these rings. My roles as a son, a student, an employee, an employer, a husband, a father, and a follower of Jesus have all shaped my understanding of the 7 Rings. And the role that encompasses them best is probably that of entrepreneur, a word derived from the Old French word *entreprendre*, which means simply to undertake, typically something new and unknown, such as an ocean voyage or wilderness expedition.

So I would like to invite you to journey with me as I share the 7 Rings of Life and how they help me make the most of my life. Believe me, the last thing I want to do is offer another self-help, motivational book. We have plenty of those already, from the business-oriented get-rich-quick types by CEOs and celebrities to the more faith-based ones by pastors, counselors, and theologians. In my humble opinion, most of these books are too long, too wordy, and don't often connect faith with business, politics with community, or financial success with humble service. And rarely are they authored by someone who has worked in all these areas. Many of us could benefit from a field guide, an overview of life's terrain and how to navigate it smoothly. I wish I could have had such a guide when I was younger so now I'm simply sharing some of the ideas and lessons I have learned through the years.

That's the purpose of this book.

I'm not writing it to be famous or make money or attract the attention of the media. I'm writing it to help people in ways that others helped me. And all the net sales proceeds from this book will be donated to a variety of worthy causes through the Brian Watson Foundation. As you'll see, and as I hope I demonstrate in the pages to come, this book is about giving—to yourself, to your Creator, to your spouse, to your children, to your community, to our nation, and to our planet.

MAKING THE 7 RINGS WORK FOR YOU

My goal is to simply share the real and sometimes painful experiences of someone who was raised in humble means, experienced the pain of two parents getting divorced, witnessed the unexpected death of his stepfather in front of him, built a successful commercial real estate investment company, and is a father of three and husband of almost two decades. I hope to convey the experience of a common man who has worked hard to pursue and reap the benefits of the real American Dream, and who works every day to help improve others' lives and to create opportunities for everyone around me.

I sincerely hope you can be encouraged by my experiences, and that you may be able to create a model for your own life through some of the ideas I will share. Though your structure and prioritization, or even the rings themselves, may be different than mine, I challenge you to consider what they should be, thoughtfully and even prayerfully, as you implement them to create a life full of rich experiences, blessings, and the opportunity to love and serve others in love.

The last time I checked, none of us humans are getting off this planet alive in a physical form, as we each have a finite life to live in our current state. The question you must answer confronts you on a daily basis: what will you do with your life in the coming minutes, days, months and years? What do you want your legacy to be, and how does that include leaving this world a little better than you found it?

As I said, I don't have all the answers, or even most of them, but I can come alongside you and share how I have come to answer those big questions and the actions I have taken as a result. If nothing else, I hope this book provides you with some thought-provoking, perspective-shifting ideas from another person who is traveling on this journey of life with you.

As you proceed through this book, you will notice seven quotes to consider under the heading "Ring of Truth" at the end of each chapter. They are designed to inspire you and to ignite your own sense of each ring and its importance in your life. From ancient scholars to modern leaders, these are quotes I especially appreciate and have curated for that chapter's focus. By no means are these the only ones that could apply, but they are ones I believe you'll find especially relevant and helpful.

At the end of each chapter, you will also find a few key questions and application exercises labeled "Ring of Honor." Obviously, you will reap the most benefit if you actually take the time to complete them. I know we are all busy, but these questions are designed to have you think about the material and your own life situation in a deeper way. I'm convinced it's better to be "proactive" rather than "reactive" in the world, and such planning will help you truly design your own life in a more proactive way. You are the architect of the life you want to live, and these questions and exercises will provide you with tools for your blueprint.

In addition, I encourage you to consider discussing the exercise questions with a friend, your significant other, or small group. They may help to spur some conversations that will not only benefit you, but could also deepen your friendship between each other, by allowing you to discuss topics and ideas that are often challenging to face. Whatever method you use, however you interact with the ideas that follow, I hope this book provides a positive impact in your life.

Your life is a precious and temporal gift that should not be squandered. Every minute and day counts, so make these the best that you can, as you only live once. With your own 7 Rings to guide you, you can make the most of your time here on earth.

Ready to get started? Then let's look at the First Ring.

CHAPTER 1

THE 7 RINGS:
FROM DANTE TO DENVER

"Consider your origins: you were not made to live as brutes, but to follow virtue and knowledge." | **Dante Alighieri**

Looking back, I felt like my life had fallen off a cliff. One minute I was gaining ground toward new heights. In the next, the ground gave way beneath me, and I was left barely clinging to a sheer rock wall by my fingertips.

The economic downturn of 2008 left me and my company, Northstar Commercial Partners, like so many others, in a precarious place. I had worked my entire life to start Northstar, which I finally launched in 2000, and we were quickly becoming a large commercial real estate investment company with millions of square feet of office, retail, and industrial properties that we owned throughout America. But suddenly it all seemed in jeopardy.

The banking, mortgage, and real estate markets took some of the hardest hits, and because those all figure directly into our business, we were squarely in the line of fire. Loans were called in from lenders who felt insecure. Other institutions closed altogether. Some of our tenants cancelled their leases while others simply disappeared, bankrupt and unable to pay us.

But I had worked too hard to get to the level of success Northstar had achieved. I couldn't simply give up, sit back, watch my dreams go down in flames. So together with our company's legal counsel, who just happens to be my beautiful wife Patricia, we fought to survive. Each day and into the night, and sometimes the early morning, Patricia and I met with clients as well as our lenders, reviewed our properties, researched others, addressed foreclosure actions by lenders on a few of our investment properties, and spent thousands of hours going over our financials trying to develop solutions.

Our frantic efforts remind me of the scene in *It's a Wonderful Life* when Jimmy Stewart and Donna Reed, as the newly married George and Mary Bailey, are leaving Bedford Falls on their honeymoon. Only there's a run on the banks due to the stock market crash, and they end up going back to the Savings and Loan, using their honeymoon cash to pay customers and stave off Mr. Potter. As the clock strikes 6 o'clock, they lock their office doors and realize they were miraculously still solvent—with all of two one-dollar bills.

Patricia and I lost all of our personal wealth during this period trying to keep all our employees paid and paying settled deficiencies on investment loans I had personally guaranteed. In fact, by the end we were literally millions of dollars in the hole, without much hope of digging out. I lost sleep and neglected my health as my wife and I dipped into all our personal savings to pay employees, creditors, and other obligations just to stay afloat. We had committed to keep going as long as we possibly could and refused to consider bankruptcy an option even though attorneys and many other people said we should do so and start over fresh with no debt. Maybe it was my pride and optimistic personality that wouldn't allow me to quit, but I like to think it was the result of my moral values and spiritual faith.

Maybe one of the reasons I clung to my faith and trusted we would survive the recession stemmed from my upbringing and the obstacles I had already overcome. While I had experienced countless blessings, I had also suffered several heartbreaking losses—including my parents' divorce, the death of my beloved stepfather, and the economic struggles that came from growing up in a middle class, hard-working family. You see, nothing was ever handed to me on a silver platter. I had worked so hard for so long, and it seemed that Northstar was at last on the brink of incredible success. And then the recession sent us spiraling downward, losing all the momentum we had gained.

Each day grew bleaker and bleaker, and soon it felt like we would have no choice but to close our doors. But I refused to give up. It's simply not in my DNA. I didn't know how, but I had to believe somehow, some way, we would survive this financial and personal ordeal. And not only survive it—but learn and grow from it.

Such a hopeful attitude may sound foolish to you, but let me back up and describe how I became, as I like to call it, an optimistic realist. Out of my past experiences, I developed the 7 Rings, and as the stormy waters began rising above my head, they were put to the test.

HUMBLE ORIGINS

I was born in Middletown, New York, a picturesque small town about two hours northwest of The Big Apple. The year was 1971, and my parents, Carol and Bob Lambrigger, owned and operated Russell Brook Campground, a hunting preserve and rural campground, catering mainly to people seeking a break from the city. They raised pheasants, bred and showed bird dogs, built riding stables, and worked from sun-up to long after sunset taking care of a hundred campsites. This included mowing lawns, cleaning bathrooms, maintaining the swimming pool, running a small general store, conducting trail rides and hayrides for campers, and so much more. To say my parents were hardworking is an understatement; it was in their blood, and they passed this work ethic on to me.

Shortly after her birth, my mother was adopted into a family in Brooklyn. It was later suspected that her mother died during childbirth, and her grieving father put her up for adoption. Nothing more is known of her biological parents, although she grew up in a rich tradition with Jewish family members.

My father, on the other hand, knew his mother immigrated to America from Denmark, and his father came to this country from Switzerland. Like so many immigrants in the early 20th century, these two left everything they knew, including their family and friends, in pursuit of the American Dream. Because of their sacrifices, I am an heir to the dreams they planted and nurtured and have been blessed to see many of them come to fruition.

After landing in the U.S., my grandmother worked in the sweatshops of New York City as a milner making hats, while my grandfather was a hard laborer, boxer, and small business owner, eventually founding Lambrigger Moving Company. In fact, he met his future wife, my grandmother, while moving a piano for her. Unfortunately, I never met my grandfather as he died of a heart attack before I was born. I was fortunate to meet my grandmother, and to this day I enjoy baking homemade Danish cookies with my kids each Christmas, a family tradition she passed down to us.

After many years of working very hard and saving as much money as possible, my father's parents moved to Roscoe, N.Y., in 1930 to build the "Little Switzerland of America," which consisted of a few cabins along the Beaverkill River on Old Route 17. Soon travelers, outdoorsmen, and fly fishermen rented these cabins on their visits through the Catskill Mountains, and the place enjoyed a long history of operation.

Maybe it's his entrepreneurial spirit, but I've always felt a connection with my grandfather, Constantine "Connie" Lambrigger. To this day, I keep an old black and white picture of my grandfather's moving truck in my office, my grandmother standing in front of the old vehicle, with a sign that reads "Beer—15 ¢." It is a reminder of the hardworking roots of self-sacrifice that my family came from, the history and genes of which still run through my blood.

Maybe their examples explain why I couldn't simply give up my dream when the economy collapsed and threatened to take me down with it. I come from strong stock, who know what hard manual labor means and are always willing to work our hardest, especially in tough times. No one in our family was ever financially rich, but rather we were rich in the blessings of hard work, integrity, positive can-do attitudes, family, and community.

CHANGE IS CONSTANT

Like many people, I've had my share of devastating disappointments and trials with perhaps the first occurring when I was around eight. After 21 years of marriage, my parents decided to divorce. Needless to say, their breakup was very traumatic for me. Some of the fights, screaming, and arguments between them remain vivid in my memory still. Maybe my devoted commitment to family grew from seeds planted during this time. Based on their relationship, I knew one day I wanted my own family to be closer, kinder, and more loving.

When my parents separated and my father moved out of our home, my mother was left to run the campground. Overwhelmed by the responsibility, she hired a local man named Bill Watson to help oversee the operations at our campground. Bill worked at a local quarry, cutting stone in the Catskill Mountains. His nickname was the "Stone Duster" and he was a strong, capable man. After taking the job with us, he worked long hard days as there was so much to do to help in such an operation. Then one day my mother invited Bill to stay and eat dinner with us, and after several months of him occasionally joining us for a meal, she invited him to stay with us instead of making the long drive back to his place.

It wasn't long then before they became a couple and soon married. I liked Bill and he treated me well. I also liked the kind, respectful, loving way he treated my mother. Not long after they started dating, Mom and Bill began discussing the possibility of a big move. Bill had a severe history of asthma, which was only aggravated by the climate of the Northeast. One of the main reasons for a move was to find a drier, cleaner climate to help reduce the growing number of his frequent asthma attacks.

In 1981, we moved to Montrose, Colorado. Their selection was based partly because they had visited Southwest Colorado to hunt for elk and thought it the most beautiful place they had ever seen, and in part because my mother had a friend in the area who wanted to build a large residential project that Bill could help develop, as he had construction experience.

On the night we finally arrived in Colorado, we learned that the development, which had planned to hire Bill, was not moving forward. I remember my mother and Bill discussing if they should stay in Colorado, or move to Phoenix, Arizona, where one of Bill's brothers lived. After much consideration, they decided to try and make a life for themselves in Colorado, and I'm so glad they did.

After deciding to stay in Colorado, Bill established his own construction company. By this time I was a boy on the cusp of adolescence and old enough to help Bill with this new venture. This allowed me to learn about real estate first-hand, literally from the ground up. Though most of his projects were refurbishments of existing buildings, we also constructed some new buildings as well. Whether it be laying brick or stone, making a new cement patio, building an addition to a home, we worked long hard hours together. My main role was to carry bags of cement, mix the concrete so he could lay stone, and complete a host of other manual jobs; consequently, I learned a tremendous amount about work ethic, having your word be your bond, and the satisfaction of starting a job and finishing it with a quality result.

As I worked for Bill during my summer vacations from school and on the weekends, he told me that one day I would appreciate all I was learning: how to build with my own hands, how to envision and to create, and especially the value of working hard. Once again, the seeds were planted for what would become the 7 Rings. Hard work, self-sacrifice, entrepreneurship, and the desire to build something of lasting value were all developed in me from a very young age, through the wonderful example of my parents.

During this time I grew especially close to Bill. In fact, after a few years I asked Bill to adopt me, changing my last name to Watson. After settling in Colorado, we were finally a happy family, and enjoyed hunting, fishing, camping, hiking, riding horses, and spending vacations together. We built our own house as a family, literally nailing boards, stuffing insulation, and laying brick and stone by hand. My mother still lives in this same house now 33 years later, and each time I visit home I'm reminded of all the wonderful memories we built there together.

Overall, life was good even as I began to navigate the turbulent waters of being a teenager. Although we had never regularly attended church together before moving to Colorado, we started to do so. Bill eventually became a deacon in the Montrose Community Christian Church, and for the first time in my life, faith became a priority in our lives.

A few years later, in August 1985, my mother and Bill decided to increase our family by adopting a little girl from South Korea. My older sister Lisa lived back East, and my other sister Cindy would soon be graduating from high school and leaving for college. Our family's new addition, only two and a half, became my sister Amanda, and I continue to cherish our relationship and love her like all of my other siblings. One year later, I learned I would soon have yet another new sibling. At the age of 42, my mom was pregnant! Yes, indeed, the only constant in life is change.

DEVASTATING LOSS

On a frosty January day in 1988, I was getting ready for school when Bill asked me to complete some additional chores. Already in a grumpy mood that day, I balked. Bill and I had one of our rare arguments, and we both left the house with it unresolved. Feeling badly about how I had acted, at basketball practice that evening I bought Bill a team t-shirt as a way of apologizing. He still wasn't home when I went to bed, and I left the t-shirt and a note on the counter for him. Little did I know, he would never read my words or wear that shirt.

Later that night my mom rushed in and woke me, desperately needing my help. Upon walking out to our kitchen, I saw Bill bracing himself against the counter with both arms outstretched, where inhalers and various medicine bottles were strewn before him. He was struggling to breath, gasping for air, with the sound of each raspy breath being forced through his throat.

Apparently, he had gone to a meeting in Grand Junction that afternoon, about an hour away, at a client's house. The home included several pet cats, and Bill's exposure to them triggered a severe asthma attack. Rather than heading to the nearest hospital, Bill decided to make the hour drive home. By the time he had reached our door, the asthma attack was in advanced stages.

Upon seeing him struggling, I helped carry Bill to the car so my mother could drive him to the Montrose Community Hospital. Soon after they drove away, my mother frantically pulled back into the driveway as Bill could not breathe since his diaphragm was further constricted as he sat in the passenger seat next to her. So I helped to carry Bill back into our house, and minutes later as we waited for the ambulance, he collapsed on the floor in front of me.

These memories remain so vivid. I remember the medics finally arriving, the mad dash to the hospital, and then the moment the doctor came out of the hospital room to inform us Bill had died. Upon hearing the news, my mother collapsed into my arms, weeping that her beloved husband was so unexpectedly taken away from her. Being only 16, I did not know what to say or do, so I simply held her. Everything about that night seemed surreal, too painful to process, wrenching.

For a long time afterward, I felt a gaping hole in my heart and soul, and if you have ever lost a close loved one, you know what I mean. Many months after his death, I would sit alongside Bill's grave, weeping, while other days I hoped he would walk through our front door and we'd all be a happy family together again. But he was gone.

NEW BEGINNINGS

After Bill passed away, I had to grow up very quickly. My mother enrolled at Mesa State College at age 42, in hopes of securing a college degree so she could support us financially, and I took on the role of being the man of the house, taking care of my younger sister and brother. This was not easy on me, especially juggling all my other commitments: bagging groceries at the Montrose City Market, raising animals to show and sell at our county fair, playing sports, and serving as president of The Honor Society and Future Farmers of America (FFA), as well as our high school student body.

Maybe keeping "busy" helped me to deal with losing Bill and all the pain dammed up inside of my heart. Maybe this is one of the reasons I still keep busy to this day, as I know nothing different. But at the time, juggling so many demands was simply all I knew. I suppose I had a choice, but it didn't feel that way. I couldn't imagine leaving my mom at such a time or abandoning my younger siblings. They needed me and I had to do what needed to be done. And I wanted to make Bill proud, to live up to the example he had set for me. He was such a good man, and that's what I now aspired to be more than ever. My life wasn't about me any longer, but rather about being as strong and effective as I could be for those around me.

After graduating from Olathe High School with 52 other kids in 1989, I applied and was accepted at the University of Colorado (CU) at Boulder. This institution of approximately 20,000 students was a bastion of diverse and liberal thought, which encouraged me to question, and frankly deny my Christian faith even more. I'll tell you more about my crisis of faith in the next chapter, but for now just know that my life did not get easier at college.

In order to attend college, I had to work and secure enough scholarships to pay for it, as my mother was in no position to help fund my education. I remember my first job in Boulder was shoveling horse stalls and cleaning a barn north of town, something very familiar from my time living on the Western Slope of Colorado. Given my participation in school programs, strong academic performance, and community involvement during high school, I was able to secure many scholarships, which I augmented with work to support myself all through my college career. From the time I was very young, I've always had to work hard at a job. When I left home at age seventeen, those jobs had to support me financially because I did not receive money from my parents.

One of the scholarships helped transform my life when I was accepted to the President's Leadership Class at CU. This program accepted about 60 students from throughout the country, all leaders in their high schools in some way. Not only did this provide a scholarship to help me pay for college, the program taught me some very valuable skills about leadership, working with people, and understanding people who may be different than me. Without a doubt, it helped me to begin developing my own method of leadership, which I continue to improve upon to this day.

After graduating from CU Boulder in 1993 with a Bachelor of Science Degree with an emphasis in real estate, I traveled to upstate New York to spend a summer with my biological father before I was supposed to leave for an assignment in Africa with the Peace Corps. Though I did not have much of a relationship with him after moving to Colorado, I decided to reach out to my father after Bill's passing, when I went to college. I did this partly because of the sudden loss of Bill and the realization that I should get to know my biological father before something happened to him, and partly because I was curious about what he was like. We gradually rebuilt our relationship after many years, and are close to this day.

While visiting my father after college, I sold residential real estate for his brokerage office in the very small town of Roscoe, New York. This was a great experience for me, as I began to learn how to work with people. I also saw how dedicated my father was to his community, buying flowers and planting them on Main Street, hosting chicken barbeques for the local fire department fundraisers, and serving in his local church.

When I was a boy living with him, my father was not a person of faith, but in the years after my parents' divorce, he had remarried a woman named Hazel who was one of the most amazing women of faith I have ever met. As a small example, Hazel met a young woman one day who was recently married. Upon finding out that this new bride did not have enough money for a wedding ring, Hazel took off her own and gave it to her! Needless to say, Hazel had a transformational effect on my father, who eventually became a sincere follower of Jesus, and in addition to helping me and my father grow closer, she also encouraged me on my own journey of faith. To this day, she remains one of the most Christ-like and peaceful people I have ever met and remains a model for me of how I should love and serve others.

My father's parents had moved to the small town of Roscoe to become business owners in pursuit of the American Dream in 1930. Since then the Lambrigger name had become synonymous with trust, hard work, a "can-do attitude," and dedication to making the community better. I learned that if I walked into a store without my wallet, people would be happy to let me take my items with me, knowing without a doubt that I would be back to pay for them. This kind of community trust resonated with me as I grew to become a man, as a person's word should truly be their bond.

Unfortunately, my assignment with the Peace Corps was rescinded a few months prior to my departure date. They denied my service due to an allergic reaction to bee stings from when I was very young. This was hard for me to accept, as I had always wanted to serve in the Peace Corps since I was a young boy. It was just one more unexpected, deeply disappointing blow.

Once again it felt like the rug had been pulled out from beneath me so I decided to move back to Colorado to pursue a career in commercial real estate. If I couldn't serve in the Peace Corps, I would join the business world. Upon arriving back in Colorado, I called every major commercial real estate brokerage firm to see if they would hire me. No one was hiring inexperienced people like me at the time, due to the poor condition of the real estate market.

Undaunted, I told one of these companies, Cushman and Wakefield of Colorado, that I would work for free. All they had to do was give me a phone and cubicle, and they would not regret it. They said "thanks but no thanks." After repeatedly contacting them for weeks, I finally told them I planned to come down to their offices on the following Monday and start working at no cost to them. I guess this was enough, as they finally gave in and offered me a job, at a pay rate that was almost like working for free.

Later I learned that such persistence and an undaunted attitude are attributes they look for in new brokers, as the business is difficult, and you have to be able to continually cold-call companies to earn their business. The training at Cushman and Wakefield continues to serve me well today, as I will still call anyone for anything, and I still like building relationships that often start with a simple phone call or handshake.

HUNT AND KILL

Working at C&W was challenging and invigorating, but I struggled financially for some time. Though the company gave me a small draw against future earnings at the beginning, they quickly pushed me to be 100% commission based. This means that I would not get paid unless I went out to "hunt and kill" in order to eat financially. This was done by cold-calling tenants, usually starting with a stack of marketing flyers, knocking on the doors of each company of an office building, and working my way down each hallway and each floor.

This was not a job for someone who was shy or unsure of themselves, as the competition to secure the tenant representation assignment was fierce, and the deal negotiation after that would be even more challenging. In the end, you hoped to have your client sign a lease, and then you finally earned a commission. This commission was then shared 50% with the house (Cushman and Wakefield), with your team (junior brokers usually received a small part of this, with the majority going to the senior brokers on your team), and then with the government in the form of taxes.

In the end, you were left with some money, though a whole lot less than what you started with. You also had to learn to save this money, to make it last until the next deal closed. Many younger brokers would create "golden handcuffs" for themselves by buying expensive cars or big houses when they got paid a large commission check, thinking that many more would be coming right behind it. Sometimes they would have dry spells between commissions, which can be very challenging, but either way they had to keep pushing to meet the lifestyle and bills they had incurred.

The environment at C&W taught me how to build rapport with people quickly, how to call anyone for anything, how to negotiate, how to be independent and strong, and how to save my money so it would last through the slower periods. The experience was invaluable, and I earned an "MBA" while being a commercial real estate broker, though I never received an actual piece of paper for my degree. I am truly grateful for this hands-on training in survival of the fittest and the "art of the deal."

Even now, I still enjoy working with brokers as we often engage them to market buildings we own throughout America, which are currently located in seventeen states, including New York, California, Washington, Alabama, and Texas.

Soon after joining Cushman & Wakefield, I decided to buy a small condo in a historic building in the Capitol Hill Neighborhood of Denver. I have always appreciated historic buildings, especially those that have withstood the test of time. Even though I was able to buy my first real estate asset at age 21, I did not have enough money for furniture, or much else for that matter. I slept on an old used mattress on the floor as my bed with no frame—I remember it vividly. Lime green in color, it was called "The Young Married Set" with a dated 1970's print on it.

I would often eat my dinner out of the same pots that I cooked them in. Not having a lot of disposable income, I would intentionally skip eating breakfast and lunch, and then go to an "all you can eat buffet" (usually Chinese or Indian food) late in the afternoon just before the restaurant closed. I would eat one very large meal at that buffet, until my stomach would hurt, which would be my only meal for the day. Though this was not healthy, it was what I had to do to stretch the limited money that I had. When I wasn't eating at a buffet, I would eat packages of inexpensive ramen noodles or other low-cost fare.

After many months of working at C&W, I finally saved enough money that I could make my first new large furniture purchase. I decided to buy a dining room table, as I enjoyed cooking, and loved long conversations with friends at the dinner table. I remember that we would sit for hours at that table after dinner parties, partly because I did not have a lot of other furniture to sit on at the time. During this stage, I taught myself how to cook, and have since enjoyed doing so, which helped me meet the woman of my dreams.

BUILDING DREAMS

In 1996, I met Patricia Lee Uhrig, and almost immediately we began building dreams together. We married almost one year to the day after meeting each other. She was putting herself through law school at Florida State University as a single parent and shared many of the same values, beliefs, and motivations that I had come to see in myself. We began putting down roots in the Denver area, and eventually we would add two more—our sons—to our family. My career had taken off at C&W, and we were able to buy our first home and enjoy a few of life's small luxuries, though much of our money was spent paying off student loan debt that we had used to help fund our respective college degrees.

But soon the day came I knew I would eventually reach. In 2000, I decided it was time to take a step backward from the comfortable lifestyle we were building, and take a giant leap forward in establishing our own company, Northstar Commercial Partners. In those first days of starting a new business, I did not know anything about the laws, regulations, how to handle personnel, or even how to raise capital for my investment deals.

We started with a few hundred square feet of office space, completely self-funded with no family or outsider investments, in a historic building on Larimer Square in the Lower Downtown (LoDo) Neighborhood of Denver. Of course the area was not as trendy as it is now, but it was a good place to plant the seeds of one's dreams. From selecting a name, logo, furniture, and every other aspect it was a challenge, but it was extremely exhilarating. We had the opportunity to literally create something from nothing, to place our fingerprint upon what could be.

Looking back, I am sure many people thought we were crazy, or that we would fail soon. To me, true failure would have been not to follow this calling of fulfilling our dream. It was the feeling of knowing exactly what I supposed to do in this world: to create, to build, to see value where others thought it did not exist, in order to create opportunity and empower others. Coming from a family of hard working, humble entrepreneurs, I had a deep calling to create a company myself, and it was the right time to do it.

After eight years of working extremely long hours to build the company, the Great Recession hit and everything we had worked so hard to achieve was in jeopardy. But during those late nights when Patricia and I would work on every aspect of the business together, I learned something about what matters most. Whether you call them "priorities" or "life-work balance," these lessons became what I now want to share with you here: the 7 Rings of Life. One friend tells me they are the antithesis of Dante's *9 Circles of Hell,* and I certainly hope so. The events from which they emerged sometimes felt like hell, but the 7 Rings are about living life to the fullest, with peace, purpose, and passion every day. They are also about putting your stock in the eternal things that matter most, not the temporary fleeting things that the world often puts forth as the most important.

During this period it was like trying to navigate a gauntlet or mine field: we took hits, we bled, we cried, and we even lost limbs. What could have destroyed our marriage and forced us to give up in despair, however, only drew Patricia and I closer together, reinforcing our resolve to make it through this difficult time together. True, we suffered as some banks foreclosed on three of our investment properties, and also when a manager of a company we invested in was unscrupulous and didn't pay the IRS, which we then had to pay personally. Unfortunately, we lost people who said they were our friends when times were good, but who ran when things became challenging. These were tough times, but I am grateful for them, as they gave us clarity of purpose, strength, resolve, a belief in each other and our marriage, and a commitment to do what's right even when it's not easy to do so.

As you may have guessed, we did survive the Great Recession and subsequent economic crash, but sometimes I'm still not sure how. Actually, I am sure how, and it has to do with the First Ring—a personal relationship with God and its priority in my life. That's what we'll explore in the next chapter. Before we do, however, I encourage you to take a few minutes and read through the quotations that follow. After reflecting on them, take a few more minutes and journal your response to at least one of the exercise questions. Trust me, you'll be glad you did!

RING OF TRUTH
7 QUOTATIONS TO CONSIDER

"The true entrepreneur is a doer, not a dreamer." | **Nolan Bushnell**

"Always make your future bigger than your past." | **Dan Sullivan**

"The greatest solution of all is to live and work in partnership with yourself, your family and friends, your work and community, your nation, your world, nature, and spirit." | **Marc Allen**

"The origin of innovation and entrepreneurship is a creative mindset." | **Michael Harris**

"Inspiring someone else to follow their dreams is the hope of anyone who has the courage to follow their own." | **Dawn Garcia**

"A man must be big enough to admit his mistakes, smart enough to profit from them, and strong enough to correct them." | **John C. Maxwell**

"Success is walking from failure to failure with no loss of enthusiasm." | **Winston Churchill**

RING OF HONOR
QUESTIONS FOR REFLECTION

How would you describe your life's greatest challenge or crisis? How did you handle it? What impact does it continue to have on your life?

_____

_____

_____

_____

_____

What five major events in your life have shaped you the most? How have they influenced you and the kind of person you are right now?

_____

_____

_____

_____

_____

What motivates you to pursue your dreams through adversity? Family? Success? Money? Material possessions? Security? Something else? Be honest with yourself about what it is you really want from life.

_____

_____

_____

_____

_____

How do you handle the losses in your life? Have you grieved your life's major losses? How have you processed their effect on your life?

_____

_____

_____

_____

_____

How willing are you to take risks in your life? On a scale of 1 (not at all) to 10 (all the time) rate your openness to stepping out in faith?

_____

_____

_____

_____

_____

CHAPTER 2

THE FIRST RING:
DIVINE DESIRE

"Faith is taking the first step even when you don't see the whole staircase." | **Martin Luther King, Jr.**

Faith, the personal and spiritual kind, remains difficult to talk about in our world today. On one hand, one's spiritual beliefs are said to be too personal, too subjective and unique to each individual, too intimate to discuss with most people. The old adage about not discussing religion and politics with strangers still holds true today. Because if you do, in most cases, it's sure to cause conflict and disagreement.

On the other hand, what a person believes—truly believes, deep inside—directly affects their motives, choices, and actions, all of which impacts how they relate to everyone and everything around them. You see, our core beliefs about God, even whether one exists, impacts how we face everything we encounter in life—especially adversity.

The big questions of life are nothing new and often even seem as familiar as clichés: Why am I here? What's my purpose in life? What is life all about? And why doesn't it seem to make sense consistently? And the really big one, of course: If there's a good and all-powerful God in charge, why do we suffer so much in this life?

Answering these questions is more than I can tackle in this book. And, in fact, I don't need to tackle them for you—you're already in the middle of your own spiritual journey, whether you call it that or not. Sure, I'm sharing my experiences and the dynamics that shape what I believe, what I'm calling the 7 Rings of Life, but I offer them to you merely as a way of viewing the events, people, and moments that shape your life. I'm convinced what you believe about God is undeniably central to all the other Rings orbiting your life.

WITH OR WITHOUT YOU

While my parents' divorce left my world shaken, I was too young to have a substantial, fully formed faith. After my mother married Bill, however, our family began attending church together, and I started learning more about God and the Bible. With the breathtaking beauty of the San Juan Mountains of Colorado (shown on the cover of this book) all around me coupled with the way Bill had adopted me and loved me as his own son, it wasn't hard for me to imagine God as the source. It certainly made sense that a spiritual force beyond what we could explain through science was behind creation. Plus, I had moments when I could sense God's presence, when something in me, my soul perhaps, felt alive and connected to something much larger than myself and this world.

However, when Bill died so unexpectedly from that terrible asthma attack, my growing faith quickly crumbled. Bill was such a good man, a loving husband and devoted father. In fact, I still usually refer to Bill as my father, as I have never liked the term "stepfather" and because he treated me as his own son. I certainly loved him as my own father. Which made it all the more painful to lose him. I had already lost one father's presence in my life through my parents' divorce. To have to lose another seemed beyond unfair. It seemed cruel, uncaring, and indifferent.

Within days of Bill's passing, our church's pastor came to the house to express his condolences, to provide support, and to pray with us. As a sixteen year old trying to adjust to such an immediate devastating loss, I remained broken and angry. As I sat there waiting for Bill to walk in the door, hoping that he never left us but knowing he had, it felt like my heart had been ripped from my chest. I wanted nothing to do with the pastor or his well-intended attempts to comfort my family and me.

I might not have admitted it at the time, but I was furious at God. What kind of God would let Bill die at such a young age? Why did my father, who did so much good for so many people, have to die while thousands of criminals and murderers continued to live? How could a just and good God take my father and best friend away, when child molesters, murderers, and evil people still roamed free?

Nothing about my father's untimely death made sense.

Any sense of stability, harmony, and hope for the future had been ripped out from under me. I went from being a beloved son with everything going for me to a lonely young man who had to become the man of the house for his mother and younger siblings. Needless to say, I struggled with God and with the concept of faith in general after that. If this was the way God worked in people's lives, then why should I trust him? Was there even a God at all? Did he even exist? It sure seemed like he didn't care much at all in light of Bill's unexpected death.

I remember sitting in my truck on many days near Bill's newly dug grave just west of Montrose with a commanding view of the San Juan Mountain Range listening to U2's "With or Without You." Bono's haunting voice expressed my lament and left me sobbing, unable to imagine how I would ever be happy again. Honestly, even as I write this, tears well up in my eyes, as if I were back in that desolate moment, lonely, scared, angry, and very heartbroken. It remains one of the most painful times of my life, and if you've lost a beloved friend or family member, you understand what I experienced.

A REAL EDUCATION

We all have losses in life, and I realize now every person suffers and grieves throughout their lives. The irony, of course, is that even though such pain and grief is universal, it makes us feel more alone than ever. Death is not easy to deal with, and it can make an imprint on your heart and soul for many years to come. If you have not experienced the loss of someone close to you yet, then I am unsure if anything can truly prepare you for it. Though all of us experience it in time, it is one of those pivotal points that forever change you, forcing you to take stock of your life, and eventually helping to create perspective and priorities.

Almost two years after Bill's death, I remained resistant to religion and quietly angry and withdrawn from God. I had discovered a new equilibrium in my life, largely based on following my father's example of how to push through life by staying busy. At seventeen I juggled work, school, and my family responsibilities while preparing to make the giant leap to college at the University of Colorado, Boulder.

Like many university campuses, CU's environment proved to be fertile ground for sifting through my beliefs. For the first time in my life, I mingled with students from around the world from a variety of cultures, religions, and belief systems. Depending on the particular course and professor, I encountered people insisting on a scientific, rational view of our world. While I appreciated their rigorous approach and insistence on historical fact and logical, systematic conclusions, I also realized something was missing. Facts and logic are essential, of course, but so many facets of life cannot be reduced to an equation, a formula, or a handful of facts that have been developed by human deduction alone.

Picking up where my math and science classes left off, liberal arts courses such as literature, philosophy, art history, and psychology ignited my imagination and intellectual curiosity. Considering I had nothing to lose since I felt no commitment or obligation to any particular belief system, I began exploring various religions and their beliefs. I felt a freedom to compare what I knew of the Christian faith to Judaism, Buddhism, Islam, and even atheism.

Curiously enough, the result, at least at the time, surprised me. After studying many of the world's great religions and doctrines of thought, the Christian faith proved its truth to me more and more. Through this process of questioning, doubting, exploring, and experiencing various spiritual approaches to life, the faith of my parents became my own. By asking question after question, I concluded that no challenge in the past 2,000 years, or any for the next 2,000 years, could change the truth of who Jesus was—the Son of God—and what he did for humankind.

Living in the freedom to believe whatever I wanted, in an open-minded environment of liberal beliefs and multi-cultural practices, I came back to where I started with a fresh perspective and a much more personal sense of its significance to me. Maybe nothing expresses this better than these verses from T.S. Eliot's *Four Quartets*:

We shall not cease from exploration
And the end of all our exploring
Will be to arrive where we started
And know the place for the first time.

I still couldn't make sense of Bill's death, as well as so many other losses and injustices in the world, but I could no longer deny that there was a God, one I could know personally, one who loved me even though I didn't understand him or his ways. I was no longer "going through the motions," but realized that this was my journey, and that the undeniable truth of faith would be seared upon my heart, forever.

COME AS YOU ARE

I'm convinced through healthy questioning, God reveals his awesome power of love and grace to all people, just like you and me. He's more than able to handle our questions and doubts, our angers and fears, our emotional outbursts and uncertain fears. But this requires our willingness to be open to him and what he wants to do in our lives. This requires exercising faith—believing in a spiritual force that cannot always be seen or proved or measured. This requires accepting our own limitations and acknowledging our need for God's love and forgiveness.

The idea that we are all fallen and that God himself loved his creation so much that He took on human form to die a bloody, ridiculed, and painful death on a cross is simply overwhelming. And with this, God displays an endless amount of love and grace for people like us, not only in spite of, but *because* of our brokenness.

In fact, we don't have to be cleaned up and perfect before we come to him. Instead he embraces us with unconditional love as we enter his presence in a tattered state, bloody, dirty, and unworthy. We don't have to have our act together and everything figured out, resolved, and tied up with a bow. Our relationship with him is the ultimate "come as you are" party. God had accepted my anger, grief, and doubts without ever giving up on me or requiring me to discount my feelings. He knew and still knows my weaknesses, flaws, mistakes and struggles, and loves me just the same anyway.

After seeing and experiencing God's beauty, love, and massive amount of grace in the world, how could I not place him in the center of my life? Yes, losing my father was a wound I would carry for the rest of my life, but I couldn't deny the countless blessings in my life each day: a healthy body, food to eat, shelter, clothing, a loving family, and a college education. Being his creation, how could I not supply the one small act of service and love to the Creator of the Universe?

We all have a God-shaped void in our hearts and souls. The Bible tells us this truth throughout its pages. If you look within yourself and think over the best and worst moments of your life, you know this truth as well. Even in the best of times, there's still a lingering sense of something not quite enough, not quite satisfied, just out of reach. And in the hardest times, this nagging ache becomes a sharp, acute pain of emptiness and despair. Humans are spiritual beings. Even many hardcore scientists and medical researchers acknowledge an unseen dimension to our beings that is inextricably woven into the fabric of our humanity.

We often try to fill this void, this spiritual longing for meaning and fulfillment, this divine desire, with other things, including many that are bad for us. Excessive amounts of drugs, alcohol, sex, exercise, work or any other "thing" will never fill the void that was made for the Creator to be in a relationship with you. In fact, the essence of addiction is an attachment or reliance on something counterfeit to fill this vacancy within your heart. But no blissful high, grand achievement, or material possession can ever fulfill us. They may distract and entertain and numb us for a while. But ultimately, we're still left wanting more, wanting something else that remains elusive.

What we desire is a relationship with God and a sense of our identity and purpose as his creation. We want to know what we do matters and to experience some sense of transcendence beyond our daily routines and hectic schedules. We want to be more than just the sum of our roles and responsibilities. We want to be loved and accepted in ways we can't even articulate. We want to be challenged and to live up to our special gifts and unique potential.

We want to know there's more beyond this life.

This is the First Ring. If you don't start with your worldview and what you believe about life, about love, about loss, then you will struggle adding and developing the other six rings. Because the First Ring exerts a gravitational pull on all the other dimensions of your life. Even if you say you don't believe in anything, then that still creates a lens through which you see the world and your place in it. In fact, we all have a First Ring— only it might not be powerful enough to sustain us. If the primary focus of our life is wealth or fame or achievement, inevitably we find they're not enough.

So I challenge you to look within and describe your current First Ring. If you haven't explored becoming a follower of Jesus, then I encourage you to see beyond the culture wars in our country, beyond the preachers on television, and beyond your own baggage with the church you grew up in or your past history with religion. I know this is not easy. But if you truly desire to live life to the fullest, to have a wildly enjoyable, peace-filled, meaningful adventure each and every day, then open your heart to Jesus. Ask him to reveal himself and show his love to you. It may not be what you expect—in fact, it probably won't be what you expect—but if you earnestly seek him, he will not let you down.

And if you already know God and have chosen to follow his Son Jesus, then I would ask you to assess where you are on your spiritual journey. Do you feel in sync with God and what he wants for your life? Are there barriers coming between you and a closer relationship with God? Take inventory of what's really in your First Ring and clear more room so that your relationship with Jesus can fill the center of your life.

When you submit yourself to this call, I believe you become at peace with your life, and gain ultimate confidence in why you are here on this planet: "Love the LORD your God with all your heart and with all your soul and with all your strength" (Deuteronomy 6:5, NIV). If we as followers of Jesus would just be known for our love and service towards others, we would continue to transform the world for the better, just as a Jew from Galilee and a few disciples did many years ago. Compassion, love, and service—there are no laws against these, and we each can practice these daily at little to no cost.

NOTHING TO LOSE, ALL TO GAIN

Let's assume for a moment that this whole "God" and "religion" thing is completely false, and that I along with a few billion others, are "self-deceived" and "unenlightened." If so, then what have I lost by committing to follow Jesus and his example? And how much more I have gained in my love and service for others, and in appreciating beauty and service to my fellow human beings!

Left to our own devices, humans can be selfish and destructive, but in being called to a higher standard we are able to focus on serving and loving others beyond our natural inclinations. One of my heroes, U.S. President Abraham Lincoln, once said: "I can see how it might be possible for a man to look down upon the earth and be an atheist, but I cannot conceive how a man could look up into the heavens and say there is no God."

Upon my death, I am confident in meeting God through his grace and my subsequent salvation, and I hope to hear him say: "Well done, good and faithful servant" (Matt. 25:23, NIV). If I am incorrect, and there is nothing after death, then I rest well in the knowledge that my faith helped me to love and serve others while I was living. Even though this is not the natural human approach to life, I am blessed whether I am fortunate to help make a positive impact in one life or hundreds of lives.

You see, the love and service I aspire to give are not about me. They are the reflection of God's love in and for me, and this is why God is at the center of my life, as a position of anything less would be unworthy to him. If you place other temporary and potentially shifting things at the center of your life, if you place your trust in anything besides him in this life, you will not have a solid, dependable, and never changing foundation to build upon. God's truth is unchanging and eternal.

The Bible illustrates God's love, his creation story, and how we should conduct our lives. This "Operating Manual of Life" is a powerful guide to submitting yourself to his will, to serving and loving others as he has done for us. This instruction helps to redirect your life, where it is not about you, but about your love for the Father, and your love and service to your fellow human beings. This is not solely about judgment, but about massive grace, love, and forgiveness. No one is perfect and we all make mistakes. In order to relate, love, and forgive others—and have them do the same for us—requires honesty and humility.

With this attitude as my foundation, it helps to direct how I should treat others, how I should serve, and how I should love all people, especially those who may be different than me and my culture. It is powerful, and if you haven't spent any time reading the Bible, praying, or attending a church, I recommend that you try it. Faith has transformed the world, and though some have used it for destruction and their own personal gain, the real Word is positively transforming, and positively impactful for millions of lives, including my own.

YOUR SOUL'S WORTH

As you're well aware, the Christmas and Easter holidays celebrate two of the greatest aspects of Jesus' life on earth: his birth in a stable near the hills of Bethlehem and his resurrection from death. When I consider that Christ left his home in heaven and took a leave of absence from his full power and glory as the Son of God to experience human suffering and sacrifice himself so that all people might have salvation, it boggles my mind. As someone who raised sheep, cows, pigs, and horses, I know firsthand there's nothing sweet or even sanitary about a baby being born in a barn. It's about as dirty, smelly, and earthy as you can get. And being placed in a manger instead of a crib? It's as humble and basic as anyone could experience.

Then to live a life, much of it "undercover" as a carpenter's son from Nazareth, filled with loneliness, suffering, and injustice? I'm even more blown away, as I too have worked as a carpenter's son and understand how hard and demanding that work can be. And amazingly, Jesus knew what would happen all along—he knew how excruciatingly painful, how heartbreaking, how infuriating, it would all be. He knew some of those closest to him would betray him and that some whom others rejected would draw the closest to him. His willingness to serve and suffer in this way could only be motivated by love—nothing else remotely makes sense! He did not come here to spread massive judgment and destruction, but rather undying love and service to all.

Each year during the holidays, amidst the cultural trappings and feel-good decorations, I try to keep my focus on why Jesus would pay such an enormous price by coming to earth in human form. And the best answer I've come up with revealed itself one year when I was singing Christmas carols with my family at church. Up until that night, "O Holy Night" was a song I enjoyed but it was not my favorite. But then I heard the lyrics with new ears, from a fresh perspective, that year and the answer emerged so simple and clear:

> "*Long lay the world in sin and error pining*
> *Till he appear'd and the soul felt its worth.*"

That verse became the most important in the entire song—maybe any Christmas song—for me. Jesus lived and died and rose from the dead so that you and I might know our true worth, our real value as children of God! As someone who deals with property appraisals and real estate estimations of value everyday, I suddenly had a new insight into the worth of my very soul. While real estate and commercial properties' value are influenced by various factors, especially the economy, the value of the human soul is constant, fixed, and priceless. God relinquished the cherished relationship with his only Son so we could know him and spend eternity with him.

Think for a moment about the last time you felt your soul's *true* worth, all because the Savior of the Universe took on human form to save the world as the perfect and thus final sacrifice. Have you truly felt the worth of your own soul yet? I hope so, as Jesus literally allowed himself to be sacrificed so that you would.

For anyone that doesn't have faith and wonders why followers of Jesus want them to know him and follow him, too, please allow me to explain. For those committed to following the example of Jesus, it's not about drawing a line and setting themselves against the rest of the world. Each follower of Jesus has been and still is a sinner, with no exceptions. Because they know of their own shortcomings and failures, they want to share with you the true grace and love of God, that has helped to positively transform their lives, and that ensures their eternal relationship with the Creator of the Universe.

This is the Good News that drives them to share it with everyone around them. Sadly, this conversion ethic sometimes makes many non-believers feel they are being judged or are somehow perceived as being "less" or "evil" or "unworthy." Actually, the exact opposite is true, as those who follow Jesus know you are a beloved child of God, and in turn they want to love you as well. Someone's sins are not to be measured, but rather all sin is simply the separation from God. He wants to be in a relationship with you, but since a perfect being cannot be in the presence of sin, Jesus made the ultimate final sacrifice of his life so each of us could be in perfect relationship with God.

People of faith are not called to love the sinful behavior, but they are called to love you as a created being in the image of God. This is true transformation that can positively impact the world for the better if people acted more like Jesus, and less like the rest of the world. Jesus is the model we try to emulate. He loved. He served. He gave the ultimate sacrifice of dying on the cross to be that perfect sacrifice to rejoin us with God. Every sin you have committed, and every one you will commit that separates you from being with God, is washed away through the death on the cross.

This is powerful.
This is life-changing.
This is true faith in the Lord.

With God at the Center of my life it helps to provide clarity on the remaining six outer rings, as my purpose, moral framework, love, and service all emanate from this point. If you ask most people on the street what they know about Christians, they will likely tell you the things believers are against instead of the things we stand for. I wish to change this perception in this world, and first above all else to be known for my love and service to others, especially those different than me.

My job is to love everyone just as completely as Jesus loves them, regardless of their faith, belief system, nationality, sexuality, economic status, or political views. As my company's international business grows and I travel around the world, I am privileged to befriend people who are Jewish, Muslim, Buddhist, as well as those who are non-believers. I don't talk about my faith with them unless they ask, and then I enjoy having an open, non-judgmental discussion. My goal is to respect them and hope they will know I follow Jesus simply by my actions.

Unlike some foundations that can shift due to their human creation, this is a foundation stone that is unchanging and immeasurable. If you want a balanced life, then you must have a solid, bedrock foundation that won't crumble when life's storms batter you around. I encourage you to make your relationship with God your First Ring and the others will always be easier to define and balance.

RING OF TRUTH
7 QUOTATIONS TO CONSIDER

"What you are is God's gift to you, what you become is your gift to God." | **Hans Urs von Balthasar**

"You can tell the size of your God by looking at the size of your worry list. The longer your list, the smaller your God." | *Author Unknown*

"Maybe the atheist cannot find God for the same reason a thief cannot find a policeman." | **Author Unknown**

"A man can no more diminish God's glory by refusing to worship Him than a lunatic can put out the sun by scribbling the word, 'darkness' on the walls of his cell." | **C.S. Lewis**

"But I always think that the best way to know God is to love many things." | **Vincent van Gogh**

"God's gifts put man's best dreams to shame." | **Elizabeth Barrett Browning**

"I know God will not give me anything I can't handle. I just wish that He didn't trust me so much." | **Mother Teresa**

RING OF HONOR
QUESTIONS FOR REFLECTION

What's at the center of your First Ring right now? How consciously did it get there? Is this what you want to be there? Why or why not? How do you feel about placing your relationship with God at the center of your life? What has prevented you from surrendering to this choice in the past? What, if anything, keeps you from this commitment now?

_____

_____

_____

_____

_____

Have you ever placed material, shifting, or temporary things at the center of your life? How has their pursuit left you feeling about your life and its significance? In other words, are these things unchanging, truthful, and eternal regardless of the state of your health, whether you are living or deceased?

_____

_____

_____

_____

_____

If you have not thought about a relationship with the Creator of the Universe, have you have tried praying a simple prayer? Prayer is having a conversation with God, and you have the ability to open this channel of communication simply by bowing your head, closing your eyes, and beginning to talk with

God. Try it sometime, and if you already do it, commit to praying on a regular basis, even every day or several times a day.

I have found that the most powerful prayer that you can state is: "Lord, not my will but yours. I submit myself to you, and ask that your will be done, no matter what road that takes me on." I encourage you to try it. But be prepared, as this is powerful, and may lead you in areas that you never thought possible!

Do you know the true worth of your own soul? Do you feel mired in guilt, shame, fear, and self-contempt? Or as the carol describes it "sin and error pining"? Or are you truly free in the Divine Nature of God through His Grace and Love?

CHAPTER 3

THE SECOND RING:
JOINED AT THE HEART

"Happy marriages begin when we marry the ones we love, and they blossom when we love the ones we marry." | **Tom Mullen**

Within one week of meeting Patricia Lee Uhrig, I knew she would be my wife. Many people had told me that this kind of instant certainty was possible, but until it happened to me firsthand, I didn't really believe them. There was no denying, however, the powerful first impression she made on me. It wasn't so much love at first sight—even though she was (and still is) a strikingly beautiful woman. But I associate "love at first sight" with crushes and infatuations, instant attractions based on appearances and sexy attitudes.

Meeting Patricia was about something much deeper than just the lovely smile and long dark hair I first glimpsed when she walked into our office space at Cushman and Wakefield in downtown Denver. She was there visiting her best friend in Colorado from her home in Florida. From the start there was something dynamic in her presence—an energy, an attitude of kindness, a balance between knowing the harsh realities of the world and practicing the grace to bear them.

There was a sparkle in her eyes that spoke to my soul without uttering a word.

WE JUST KNEW

Though I had dated different women throughout the years, Patricia was the first and only one who captivated my heart. I suspect this was, in part, because of her selfless love for others. When we first met, Patricia was a young single mom with a four-year-old daughter, Taylor. Finding herself pregnant at a time in her life, and in our culture, when many young women chose abortion, instead Patricia felt responsible for this new life inside her. Given her strength of will and selfless love, she elected to keep her baby. As difficult to believe as it may sound, she never resented having a child so young and viewed her little girl as a beautiful gift from God.

Patricia didn't allow motherhood to dampen her determination for finishing her education and proceeding with her career plans either. She enrolled in law school, juggled a couple of part-time jobs as a waitress and bartender to support herself and her daughter, and remained as hands-on as possible with raising little Taylor. She credits the support of her parents and some good friends, but clearly Patricia is not a woman who shrinks from a challenge. As I would quickly learn, she refuses to let obstacles be anything other than an opportunity for innovation.

Clearly focused on launching her career and continuing to be the best mother she could be, Patricia didn't have much time to date or pursue romantic relationships. (All her hard work clearly paid off as she would go on to graduate second in her law school class at Florida State University, with her moot trial team winning the national title that year.) But her mindset quickly changed shortly after we met. In fact, it wasn't even a week before she and I began discussing marriage!

Our friends thought we had lost our minds, but we just laughed and let them think whatever they wanted. Somehow Patricia and I both just knew we were supposed to be together and combine our separate lives into one family. As complicated as long-distance relationships often can become, we found our connection only grew stronger.

Though she was in law school at FSU and I was a commercial real estate broker with Cushman and Wakefield in Denver, we talked for hours on the phone each night.

These conversations helped to remove some of the physical issues that can complicate and cloud a new relationship, and allowed us to get to know each other even faster with long, involved and uninterrupted phone conversations. We experienced a special emotional intimacy that didn't rely on just our physical attraction to one another. I clearly got to know Patricia in ways that I likely would not have experienced if we saw each other every week. To this day, we are able to talk with each other for long periods of time, which helps us to discuss life, business, and faith.

After having her visit me for a weekend in October, I flew to Florida after Christmas to meet her family for the first time. While there, I asked for her father's blessing and approval to marry his daughter. As a father today, I am unsure if I would have given permission to me, but that being said, her father approved. On December 31, 1996, on a boat I rented off of Key West, Florida, we became engaged when Patricia answered "yes" to the best question I have ever asked.

Two decades later, Patricia has become my best friend, partner, and confidant. Recently, we were named the "Sweetheart Couple of the Year" by a local newspaper, and a reporter wrote a full-page article about our life together. If our relationship sounds too good to be true, please understand that we have our share of problems, difficulties, conflicts, and unexpected obstacles. But through them all, our love only grows stronger because of the commitment we have to one another and the shared belief in faith that sustains us in that love. I am truly humbled each day that I get to wake up next to the most amazing, intelligent, and kind woman I know, and I feel blessed each night that I get to lay down beside her.

Though we have had our arguments like any couple may have, we always try to "meet in the middle." To us, this means each person giving as much as they can, never keeping score of who gave more or less. In doing this, we get to a middle point together much faster. We also take seriously the admonition in the Bible regarding how we handle our disagreements: "Be angry and do not sin; do not let the sun go down on your anger" (Ephesians 4:26, ESV). Though we haven't always met this particular rule 100% of the time, we know our love is strong enough to allow us to agree to disagree at times. It's the natural give-and-take that's part of every healthy relationship.

MARRIAGE BY DESIGN

As you've guessed, the Second Ring of Life is my relationship with my best friend and life partner, my wife, Patricia. Through our shared faith with God being at the Center of our lives, we have what counselors and social scientists call "common foundational grounding." This simply means that we agree on the big aspects of our life together such as what we believe about faith, moral values, our family, and our loyalty to one another.

With these central pillars supporting the structure of our marriage, we can endure life's harshest storms. This kind of bond is very important, whether we are high upon a hill or in the valley of shadows in the different seasons of our lives. No matter what we encounter, our commitment to each other and God takes precedence, provides strength, and expands our definition of love beyond just the physical or emotional needs of the moment.

Next to my relationship with my Creator, my relationship with Patricia is the next inner sanctum. Nothing else comes between this, not work, not another friend, not our children, nothing. This is by design, as I cannot be effective in my marriage and in life without being "solid" with my life partner. I know that some people have experienced tragic divorces because something worked its way between them as a married couple. So many issues seem to start small, and then become a huge wedge, and eventually a devastating divide.

Protect your heart, protect your marriage, and honor your significant other, even when—or should I say, *especially* when—you find that it's not easy to love them. And if you're not married, but want to be, then be committed to your principles about the kind of person you want to love and marry. In other words, be discerning!

Align your own life with what you believe and work on being the strongest, best version of yourself you can be. If you depend on your relationship with someone else to define you or to make you feel special, then you're setting yourself up for failure. No one can make you happy with yourself except you. Maybe you've heard this before from pop psychologists and romance-advice columns, but it's true. This is why I believe your relationship with God—which forces you to face your own faults and weaknesses—must be the First Ring of your life.

Almost every adult has baggage of some kind just from living life when they enter a serious committed relationship with another person. But if you work on yourself, on healing from past wounds, and on pursuing your God-given purpose, then you will go a long way toward being a whole, healthy individual. When two such people are headed in this same kind of positive, proactive direction, then they form a much stronger union when committed to each other. I'm convinced if you pursue relationships with honesty, purity, and integrity, your endeavors will reap huge benefits as intimacy and trust grow.

If you are divorced and still long for a relationship, then let yourself grieve what you have lost—your spouse, your partner, your marriage, and your dreams of how life would be in your future. And then be ready to take the incredibly vulnerable risk of loving someone again. Or if you know you feel called to be single, or at least single for the current season of your life, then embrace this as a gift and not a burden. Allow yourself to focus on the other people in your life whom you love—families, friends, children, and neighbors. No matter which of the seven rings we're discussing, please remember that love fuels them all.

MY TOP TEN

People often ask me for advice about their relationships or marriage. I take it as a supreme compliment and feel incredibly humbled in those moments. I make it clear that my marriage is far from perfect and that I don't have all the answers. But I do try to share what I've learned from my years together with Patricia. From these situations of being asked for the secret to our loving marriage, I've started to keep a "Top Ten" list.

So please allow me to share my "Top Ten" list and explain a little bit about each one. You may not agree with these lessons, but I hope they will at least make you pause and reflect on your own criteria for a healthy, loving marriage.

1) *Marriage takes more attention and deliberate focus than I*

imagined, but it is much more enriching and rewarding than I could have ever hoped.

Being single throughout college and while launching my career, I discovered the incredible freedom that comes from having to be accountable to no one but myself. I could basically set my own schedule in terms of when I went to bed and got up, when and where and what I ate, and what I did while I was at home in my apartment.

For the most part, I enjoyed such liberty and appreciated that I didn't have to explain or justify my preferences and habits to anyone else. If I wanted to eat leftover pizza for breakfast, I could. If I wanted to go to the gym at 5 a.m., I could. These are the simple luxuries of becoming an adult and deciding how you want to live your life.

However, there was one aspect of being single that no amount of freedom could make up for: loneliness. At the beginning of the Bible in Genesis, God said that it's not good for his new creation Adam to be alone so God made Adam a partner, a "help-mate," the first woman Eve (Genesis 2:18-22). And since we're created in his image, it's logical that we long for a deep relational connection with another human being.

When you finally find that special person whom you want to commit the rest of your life to knowing, it involves giving up some of the freedom and independence of being single. In exchange, one of the many benefits is the joy of no longer being alone but belonging to someone and creating a family of your own. But marriage still requires deliberate investments of time, energy, and engagement.

In the beginning of the relationship, it can be easy because the other person is all you can think about! After you settle into building a life together, however, it can become familiar and routine. So you have to make it the priority above all else, second only to your relationship with the Divine in the First Ring. When your spouse knows that they're second only to God, then they can relax in the security of your love and commitment. Make sure your attention level, on a daily basis, remains the same after your vows of marriage as they were before.

2) *If each person is giving 100%, it is easier to meet in the middle.*

The dynamics of a marriage relationship are fascinating. Countless books, movies, seminars, sermons, and conferences remain dedicated to studying how men and women relate and how they can strengthen and deepen their marriage. From light-hearted romantic comedies to clinical studies by university professors, virtually every source reveals that both individuals must be "all in" regarding the relationship.

Couples who marry must realize that it's not *if* conflicts and obstacles arise, it's simply *when*. If they decide to have children, their relational dynamic changes. If they change careers, move to a new area, or have to care for aging parents or loved ones, these all change the dynamics between husband and wife. Both people must be willing to give everything they have—not to the other person, which usually involves shifting or sacrificing their personal power, but to the shared commitment to love one another.

If only the husband sacrifices, protects, and leads all the time, then he will get exhausted and his wife will feel powerless. If only the wife serves, gives, and compromises all the time, then she will eventually resent her husband while he will become insecure. Similarly, no one can be right all the time. Most conflicts in marriage aren't even about being right! In my experience, many disagreements have more to do with each person feeling heard and understood, forgiven and encouraged.

When each person lets go of being right and embraces moving forward together as a couple, then solutions to problems usually become much clearer and simpler.

3) *The simple small acts of love and service every day mean much more than celebrating your love in big expensive ways, or just on Valentine's Day.*

In our culture of consumerism and constant commercials for every product imaginable, the old adage that "sex sells" seems eternally true. However, I would qualify it by saying "romance sells" more than mere sex appeal. Advertisers and businesses have learned to play on our innate human desire to love and to be loved by bombarding us with what a romance should be: beautiful people, sexy clothes, unique dates in exotic locales, expensive gifts especially jewelry and flowers, heart-melting cards, gourmet chocolates and champagne, and on and on.

But these props are not only expensive; they're unnecessary. If a relationship is just built on the feelings of infatuation and attraction, then no amount of material props can support it. As our tragically high divorce rate attests, just because you can afford romantic weekend getaways doesn't mean you have a good marriage.

Patricia and I have found that our love is best shown to one another through daily random acts of kindness, caring, and service to one another. We've become good students of one another's likes and dislikes, needs and wants. Knowing it means a lot to my wife if I cook dinner occasionally, I find the time to plan and prepare our family's meals from time to time. Likewise, Patricia knows it means a lot to me for her to listen to issues and discuss ideas related to work when I get home in the evening, especially since she's an active partner and our company's legal counsel.

Toward this goal of understanding and serving each other as a sign of your love on a daily basis, I highly recommend you read (or re-read) one of the classic relationship books, Dr. Gary Chapman's *The 5 Love Languages*. As people, we really do have different ways that we both express our love and experience it from others. Knowing and being conscientious about what your spouse needs and appreciates makes a huge difference—much more than a dozen roses or a diamond necklace.

4) ***There will always be things that get in the way of date night, and quality conversations between each other, but be sure to create the time and space for these.***

As your life together grows and becomes both more complicated with other responsibilities as well as more familiar with necessary chores and routines, you will have to let some other things take a backseat if you want to continue to build a strong marriage. The laundry will always need to be done and folded, the oil changed in the car, the kids taken to soccer practice, and reports done for tomorrow's meeting at work. But none of those will ever outweigh the importance of the person you love the most.

Of course, interruptions and distractions can crop up from time to time and derail the best plans: sick kids, a brokenhearted friend in need, and an unexpected trip to the vet just to name a few. But as soon as possible, you must make sure you find the time for one another. Our daily lives will always fill up and spill over with whatever we allow if we're not deliberate about what goes into our schedules.

You must show your spouse your level of commitment by sacrificing other responsibilities and demands on your life. This kind of sacrifice speaks louder than any poetic Hallmark card or splashy gift. The gift of time is a limited and very precious commodity. Spend it liberally on the one you love the most.

5) *Treat your spouse as if they are the most important person in the world—because they are.*

Continuing from my point above, you want to make sure your spouse knows without a doubt just how committed you are to the relationship. When you set work aside, make other arrangements for the kids to be picked up, and say no to a last-minute committee meeting, you communicate loud and clear who and what matters most.

On the other hand, if your spouse feels like they only get leftovers of your time, attention, and energy, eventually they will wonder where they stand with you. And if you don't take notice and remedy the situation, then gradually they will feel as though they are way down toward the bottom of your list—no matter what you may say.

Actions speak louder than words. Take the time to shower your beloved with the time and attention they deserve.

6) *Build quality and fun memories together, and spend your time in the moment, versus living your life in the future.*

While Patricia and I have always shared many big dreams together and worked equally hard in their pursuit, we make sure we take time to enjoy the present. It's important to plan ahead, to think about the future, and to set milestone goals for yourselves, both as individuals and as a family. But you must never overlook the joy of where you are because you're so focused on where you want to be.

Much of our lives comes down to the basic, even mundane, things that people do on a daily basis: eating, sleeping, cooking, cleaning, driving, working, and so on. If you can find ways to enjoy something as simple as preparing a meal together, tasting the rich flavors of the food, savoring a nice glass of wine with your meal, and listening to some great relaxing music, then many of that day's problems will melt away.

Planning big trips and major experiences together can be equally as enjoyable—as long as you follow through and actually take the vacation or enjoy the dancing lessons (or whatever you choose) together. Memories are the most valuable, enduring commodity you will share with your spouse and family. Even milestones like job promotions, moves, and graduations won't be remembered as much as the individual, personal, unique moments of those events. Make each moment together as rich with special memories as possible.

7) *Spontaneity creates wonderful experiences and memories. It's okay to say "yes" more often.*

Sometimes the older we get and the longer we're with our spouse, the more we lose our ability to enjoy life on the spur of the moment. While schedules and routines are necessary, keep in mind that sometimes our greatest joy in the present moment—and our most vivid memories—come from being spontaneous. Taking a weekend road trip together without a destination or simply turning up the music and dancing an impromptu tango can bring so much fun and laughter into your relationship.

Being responsible and honoring obligations and work-related responsibilities is very important. But enjoying the quality of your life on a daily basis is even more important. Follow an impulse, let go of having a plan, and surprise your spouse with that side of you that's carefree and open to adventure.

8) *Honor your spouse because they are precious. Remember that they a beloved child of God.*

In a relationship we often drift into roles and view our spouse as nothing more than our wife or husband. We lose sight of them as that strong, fascinating individual we first loved. Instead they become the mother (or father) of our children, the provider, the housekeeper, the schedule-keeper, the problem-solver, the money manager.

Don't lose sight of your partner's heart in the midst of life's daily struggles. Remember all the facets to the person who is your spouse. Try to nourish and support them not only physically and emotionally, but spiritually and creatively as well. Show them your respect by the words you use when referring to them. Serve them by putting them before yourself.

9) *Communication is key—and listening must always be the first step in the process.*

The various differences between men and women continue to be the set-up for many jokes and just as many arguments. While both male and female reflect the image of God, we are indeed wired differently on many levels, foremost biologically, physically, and emotionally. Often men want to solve problems while women frequently want to be heard and have their point of view validated. Keep in mind that listening to your spouse is more important for both genders than developing a solution or solving a problem.

Listening—truly engaging and paying full attention to another person's voice and message—sometimes seems like a lost art. We have so many voices, sounds, and interruptions vying for our attention. Even when we want to slow down and listen to our spouse, it's often difficult not to finish their sentence for them or interrupt with our proposed solution. But for real soul-baring communication to take place, you must learn how to listen and hear with your heart as well as your ears.

10) *Laugh often, judge less.*

It's easy to drift into situations where you evaluate or assess the way your spouse does something. It can be something as routine as loading the dishwasher, balancing the checkbook, or interacting with a neighbor. But when your husband or wife does something differently than you would do it—which they likely will most of the time—you must resist the temptation to correct them, judge them, or make them feel "less than" because of the way they handled the issue.

Patricia and I learned early in our marriage that laughter, often by gently poking fun at one another's quirks, draws us closer while judging, evaluating, and correcting pulls us apart. Most of the time, there's no perfect or right way to do the tasks we're faced with each day. And given the uniqueness of our personalities and experiences, most individuals will do them in their own special way.

Instead of thinking your spouse should always read your mind and do things your way, allow them the freedom to do it how they want. Unless they specifically ask for your advice or input, find a way to encourage them rather than pull them down. Better yet, make a joke about your own tendency to try and control situations—one that you can both laugh at and share.

Again, laugh more than you judge. Be silly more than you shame. And smile more than you scowl.

BEND WITHOUT BREAKING

I am sure that I will learn many more lessons in marriage during the coming years, for if we don't learn and grow, like any dormant muscle we atrophy. I hope that Patricia and I are one of those old couples you hear about, that after 60-plus years of marriage, one passes, and the other passes soon thereafter, because they can't bear being away from the love of their life. Between now and then, I plan to drink deep the years of our love and experiences, grateful for the wonderful memories and opportunity to simply hold my wife's hand.

Sadly in society today, we don't often have a lot of good role models for healthy marriages. The media and popular culture seem to celebrate infidelity, conflict, and divorce. We trend towards being a "selfie" generation, where the needs and wants of the individual override the union of two people. I may be old-fashioned, but I believe it is admirable to stay married, even when it is hard to do so. This is by no means easy, but whenever possible, try to hold onto the love between you even when it feels stretched to the breaking point. Like a willow tree in the harsh winds of a storm, bend without breaking.

The Bible describes how a man should treat his wife as the "bride of the church" (Ephesians 5:25). Growing up in church, I heard this and always wondered what it meant. But the older I've become as a married man, the clearer it seems to me. If you believe that Jesus died for the Church to be established, then a man should love his wife so much that he too is willing to die for her.

This level of love can help bind two people together in harmony, ward off threats to the marriage, and teach both spouses to honor and respect the relationship. The Bible is an operating manual that will give you strength and guidance of how you should work together. With the cultural odds stacked against you, try to spend time in the Word of God together, focusing on timeless truths that transcend cultural changes. You can beat the odds, but you must remain ever vigilant in protecting your marriage and cherishing the spouse God has given you.

RING OF TRUTH
7 QUOTATIONS TO CONSIDER

"Happy is the man who finds a true friend, and far happier is he who finds that true friend in his wife." | **Franz Schubert**

"A successful marriage requires falling in love many times, always with the same person." | **Mignon McLaughlin**

"My most brilliant achievement was my ability to be able to persuade my wife to marry me." | **Winston Churchill**

"Don't marry the person you think you can live with; marry only the individual you think you can't live without." | **James Dobson**

"There is nothing nobler or more admirable than when two people who see eye to eye keep house as man and wife, confounding their enemies and delighting their friends." | **Homer**

"Above all, love each other deeply, because love covers over a multitude of sins." | **1 Peter 4:8**

"Husbands, love your wives, just as Christ loved the church and gave himself up for her." | **Ephesians 5:25**

RING OF HONOR

QUESTIONS FOR REFLECTION

How would you describe your feelings around the concept of marriage? What has shaped these emotional associations? What marriages did you observe growing up that made an impression on you besides your parents'? Couples on television or in the movies? Others?

_____

_____

_____

_____

_____

Now how would you describe your own experience with a significant other? What challenges have you faced in your most important relationship? How did you overcome them?

_____

_____

_____

_____

_____

Which of my "Top Ten" principles resonated with you the most? Why? How does it speak to your view of marriage at this season of your life?

_____

_____

_____

_____

_____

What principle would you add to my "Top Ten" list? In other words, what have you observed about being married and sustaining a committed relationship that I've overlooked or not included here?

_____

_____

_____

_____

_____

Think about your spouse or the person you hope will be your spouse. What would you want to tell them about your hopes and fears for where you see your relationship presently? What needs to be said between you that has not been said? Consider writing a letter to your beloved and discussing some of these vital matters that need to be expressed.

_____

_____

_____

_____

_____

CHAPTER 4

THE THIRD RING:
LOVE IS THICKER THAN BLOOD

"There is no doubt that it is around the family and the home that all the greatest virtues, the most dominating virtues of human society, are created, strengthened and maintained." | **Winston Churchill**

When I said "I do" to Patricia at the altar almost twenty years ago, I became a husband and a father to a five-year-old daughter all in one affirmation. As I described in the last chapter, when Patricia and I met, I was working at Cushman and Wakefield in Denver, and she was a law school student at Florida State University. More importantly, Patricia was also the mother of a beautiful little girl named Taylor. I know without a doubt one of the reasons I fell in love with Patricia in less than a week was partly due to her strength of will and character as a single mother. I admired and respected her decision to raise a child on her own, and to put herself through law school at FSU with a toddler to raise.

Patricia's fierce compassion captivated me from the outset, as she was a woman who deeply cared about others, especially this baby, more than herself. She exemplified self-sacrifice, determination, and strength of will, but of all these worthy attributes, she exemplified love the most. She put others before herself and made the choice to do so look effortless. Knowing who she was and who she wanted to be, Patricia sacrificed so that she could love her daughter not only as a wonderful mother but also as an amazing role model of a strong woman.

Getting to know Patricia over those weeks and months of our long-distance relationship helped me glimpse her maturity and the vast depth of her capacity to love. She wasn't perfect, but she was resilient and loved Taylor unconditionally. I knew Patricia was the kind of woman I not only wanted as a wife, but the kind of woman who I would love to be the mother of my children in our family.

Our marriage and our family was founded on our shared faith, which is itself built on God's love. All the other qualities and virtues come back to love as their source. Love is truly the greatest power in the world and the most important attribute for a successful mother, parent, and spouse. The Bible is filled, from beginning to end, with the story of God's unconditional love for his people. He is the source of our ability to love because He first loved us. As a reminder of this truth, Patricia and I had "1 Corinthians 13" engraved on the inside band of our wedding rings, referencing a favorite passage (1 Corinthians 13:4-8) on love:

Love is patient, love is kind. It does not envy, it does not boast, it is not proud. It does not dishonor others, it is not self-seeking, it is not easily angered, it keeps no record of wrongs. Love does not delight in evil but rejoices with the truth. It always protects, always trusts, always hopes, always perseveres.

Love never fails.

THE COMMON DENOMINATOR

As the love grew between Patricia and me, it wasn't long after I met Taylor that she started calling me "daddy." My heart instantly melted, and I hoped and prayed I could be the father she needed me to be. There was never any sense of wondering what my life with Patricia would have been like without our daughter. Taylor was a huge part of Patricia's heart, and therefore a huge part of mine.

After Patricia and I married, we finalized a name change then a full adoption of Taylor as she was my new precious daughter. Again, it wasn't something I had to stress about. It was just the natural next step in the process of uniting our little family. The old adage tells us "blood is thicker than water," usually meaning family ties are stronger than non-family bonds. But I believe love is thicker than blood because ultimately love is the strongest glue for any family.

Looking back, I see clear evidence of how the Lord prepared my heart for a relationship with Patricia and Taylor. First, my mother had been adopted. Also, when I was young, my parents got divorced after twenty-one years of marriage. As I shared earlier, my mother then remarried a man named Bill Watson, who treated me as his own son, helped to change my last name to Watson, and subsequently adopted me just as I did with Taylor. Bill and my mother also adopted my sister Amanda, from Korea, so I've been exposed to the blessings of adoption for some time.

Today, Taylor is my daughter in every sense of the word, and I am a proud father to the amazing young woman she has become. A recent graduate from Belmont University in Nashville, Taylor is now developing her career in Nashville, and Patricia and I couldn't be prouder.

We are also proud of our two sons, Cole and Chase, and remain surprised, challenged, and ultimately delighted at the joy they add to our lives. As you've probably heard and maybe experienced, parenting sons is indeed different than parenting daughters. But the common denominator with every child is simply loving them.

Our boys are now teenagers, and Patricia and I sometimes wonder when our sweet little boys became young men. But we know that's part of the process of life. Our goal as parents is to raise children who become strong, independent individuals who leave our home well-equipped for becoming the person God made them to be. Family should be the launching pad for success.

A FIRM FOUNDATION

Clearly, I believe that being a parent to a child is one of the greatest blessings in this world. Nonetheless, you'll notice that they do not occupy the First or Second Rings. Other parents may disagree, and you might also, but I believe I love my children best when my relationship with God and my wife, their mother, precedes my relationship with them.

This doesn't mean that my kids aren't a huge priority—they most certainly are. But it simply helps me make decisions to know that I can't allow them to be at the center of who I am. Just as I am more than just a husband, I am also more than just their father. Once again, this is why my relationship with God occupies my First Ring, because it encompasses all of who I am and was made to be.

When we put our children ahead of everything and everyone else, it quickly shifts our center of gravity and destabilizes our lives. Instead of us as parents providing the safe, stable environment in which our kids can thrive, we end up reacting to them and their needs and demands. Ironically, they end up feeling insecure, uncertain, and anxious because that's how we as their parents are feeling.

I have seen some people place their kids at the very center of their existence, where the sun rises and sets on everything their children do. These people fill their lives with sports activities, school, and many other things "all for their child." In this process, they neglect their relationships with their Creator and with each other, and one day they wake up after the children have left the home, stunned that they no longer know each other.

I've seen this lead to a severe search for identity and meaning, and in some cases even divorce. This is not healthy for the child either, as they begin to develop a belief that the world revolves around them, and that their desires and wants take precedence over all others. These children often go out into the world, only to find that it doesn't cater to their every whim, and they end up being sorely disappointed and frustrated.

Patricia and I have decided that our relationship with our Creator comes first, and then our relationship with each other is in the second ring in order for us to be the healthiest, strongest parents we can be to our kids. This prioritization creates balance in our relationship with our God and with each other. It also provides stability in our home and security for our kids. Though our children often tease us about this, you can tell that they appreciate being raised on a solid foundation, especially in such an unstable, always shifting world. This gives them confidence, knowing that we love them, and that our relationships are permanent.

UNPLUGGED PARENTS

As a parent, I'm convinced giving your children an appreciation and sense of faith, a strong work ethic, true character, education, and a fire in the belly to do something meaningful with their lives is essential for healthy growth and maturity. This is not easy given the environment we all live in, but it is a good and important work. When I was young, my parents told me I would be blessed if I could impact one life for the better. As a spouse and parent, you have the unique opportunity to positively impact the lives of your children for the better. Don't waste this gift or opportunity.

Sadly, many of us have allowed technology to take the place of spending quality time with our children. I am not stating that you can't have quality time with technology present, but when the focus is solely on being entertained, you may miss out on some amazing conversations and development opportunities with your children.

Our culture's techno-fascination, including the constant presence of TV, internet, social media, tablets, and phones, often encourages us to remain distracted and disengaged from the people around us. We become so focused on selfies and videos that we overlook the need for real communication with our kids. Ironically, many parents are so focused on recording every single minute in their children's lives in order to post on social media, they're missing authentic engagement with their kids.

Each of these limits our ability to truly connect with our children and with each other. Again, these are powerful tools for education, entertainment, and enjoyment, but we must also spend time without the TV on, simply playing a board game, going for a walk together, and having conversations. Though it may be hard to believe at times, your children are yearning for you to spend time with them, to ask them about their days, and to help provide them with guidance.

A big lesson I have learned, and continue trying to learn almost every day, is to be present in the moment. Given our busy lives and ability to constantly "plug in," we can be in a room with our families and friends, but not be truly present in the moment. This is because we may be on our phones, texting others, or focused on a TV show. It's become a cliché and something of a joke that a room full of people can all be ignoring each other because they're each glued to their phone screen or mobile device.

As parents, we have set some simple guidelines with our kids. One of these is having dinner as a family together as often as possible, almost every night, without cell phones or a TV present at our dinner table. Without the distraction of new texts, tweets, and snaps, we can focus on one another and truly listen. This allows us to discuss each person's day, talk about current events, and challenge our kids to engage and discuss their own opinions.

Our kids also help us cook, set the table, and clean the dishes, all of which provide opportunities for interactions. You can learn a lot from your children, and they need to learn a lot from you, not only from their teachers at school or from TV programs. If you don't take an active role in the education of your children, other people and mediums will gladly teach them values that may be completely different compared to what you may believe. Don't allow popular culture and social media to become your children's default source of guidance and influence.

A PLACE CALLED HOME

Being a parent can be hard at times, especially when there is no "manual" for being the best parent in the world. However, there are resources available that discuss parenting skills, and how you may want to consider raising your children. As a couple, seek out these materials, and read them together. One of my favorite resources is the Bible. Along with other positive parenting resources, I find timeless truths about how to love my children in ways that build strong, healthy families as well as individuals.

No family is perfect just as no one person can be without flaws and weaknesses. But as mothers and fathers, we have considerable influence during a very crucial and formative window of time in the lives of the children we have been entrusted to love and to parent. Whether the children in our lives are biological, adopted, fostered, or simply part of our extended family and community, we all have a responsibility to lead by example.

Again, placing our relationship with God at the center of our marriage helps provide guidance on how we can be the parents we want to be. Do we make mistakes? Absolutely! Do we try our best, and also learn from these mistakes? Yes, we do. The goal is not "perfect parenting" because it doesn't exist. The goal is grace-based, God-anchored, love-fueled parenting.

So many situations will come up—everything from playground scuffles to first dates and fender benders—that will stretch you to your limits. But that's when you rely on faith and just do the best you can, loving your child the way God continues loving you. And when you make mistakes, which you will, then you humble yourself and ask forgiveness. Some of the best conversations I've ever had with my kids began when I said, "I'm sorry."

Children don't want perfection; they want love, security, stability, and protection. They want a safe place where the rest of the world and its dangers and distractions can't intrude. They want a place called home.

SHOW AND TELL

If you haven't already done so, consider that being a parent is one of the greatest blessings and responsibilities you have in this world. Unfortunately, some parents seem to view it as an obligation, an emotional and financial drain, a slow kind of relational torture to endure and simply "get through."

But this is not the parenting style we see practiced by God. You don't have to read the Bible for long to realize he knows what it's like to have stubborn, high-strung, troublesome children. And yet he still loves human beings and wants us to be the people he created us to be. He loved us enough to sacrifice his only perfect child—Jesus.

Let God's loving sacrifice empower you to become the best parent you can be, and in doing so you will have a direct and positive impact on your children that will impact them for a lifetime. Practice this everyday, and when you stumble or fall, get back up and keep going. As painful as it may be, one of the best lessons we can teach our children is how to handle disappointment and failure. They often learn more from us by watching what we do than by listening just to what we say. When they see us make mistakes, apologize, and make amends, they learn that forgiveness and grace must be part of their lives.

I encourage you to tell and to show your kids that you love them every day. This does not mean that you can only do this verbally or by lavishing gifts on them, but by spending time together, listening, and serving each other in love. My children sometimes make fun that I am always telling them that I love them and believe in them, but I think that this is vitally important.

As a young man, I was not given the chance to tell my stepfather that I was sorry for a silly argument we'd had, and that I loved him, before he was taken from our family suddenly. Don't make this mistake, and be sure that you tell your kids and your spouse that you love them, often.

The world can be filled with challenges and negativity, but hearing that you are loved with true unconditional love is empowering and positive. Though they will have their challenges, and you may have your challenges with them at times, this foundation of love and support will create a more impactful environment for each of you. Loving children is such a gift, and if you allow yourself to invest in their lives as a parent, then your life will be all the richer.

RING OF TRUTH
7 QUOTATIONS TO CONSIDER

"Raising children uses every bit of your being—your heart, your time, your patience, your foresight, your intuition to protect them, and you have to use all of this while trying to figure out how to discipline them." | **Nicole Ari Parker**

"Raising children is an uncertain thing; success is reached only after a life of battle and worry." | **Democritus**

"I think that enduring, committed love between a married couple, along with raising children, is the most noble act anyone can aspire to. It is not written about very much." | **Nicholas Sparks**

"Perhaps the soundest advice for parents is: Lighten up. People have been raising children for approximately as long as there have been people." | **George Will**

"It's hard to think of anything that is more socially beneficial than raising children well. It needs to be valued and respected, I believe by everyone in public life regardless of your political party." | **Kerry Healey**

"Train-up a child in the way he should go; even when he is old he will not depart from it." | **Proverbs 22:6**

"The family should be a closely knit group. The home should be a self-contained shelter of security; a kind of school where life's basic lessons are taught; and a kind of church where God is honored; a place where wholesome recreation and simple pleasures are enjoyed." | **Billy Graham**

RING OF HONOR
QUESTIONS FOR REFLECTION

What's at the center of your First Ring right now? How consciously did it get
If you're not a parent presently, what comes to mind when you consider the
possibility? What feelings emerge as you imagine yourself as a mother or father?

_____

_____

_____

_____

_____

If you are a parent already, how would your kids describe your parenting style?
What would your children say about you as a father or mother? What would
you say about them if they weren't present? What have you learned about
yourself from being their mother or father?

_____

_____

_____

_____

_____

Are your children at a healthy position in your relationship to your spouse, God, and your other priorities? If not, why not?

_____

_____

_____

_____

_____

What do you believe are the best things that you can provide your children with, to help enable them to be the most successful, fulfilled, and impactful people in the world?

_____

_____

_____

_____

_____

What is your greatest disappointment or struggle in your relationship with your children? Are their issues with your own parents and family of origin you need to address in order to be a better parent for your own children? What can you do to repair this relationship, so it can be the most healthy that it can be?

_____

_____

_____

_____

_____

CHAPTER 5

THE FOURTH RING:
COMMUNITY CENERED

*"The greatest gift of life is friendship, and
I have received it."* | **Hubert H. Humphrey**

I recently received a "friend" request from an old buddy from college, someone I had lost touch with over the years. Through the magic of Facebook, we were able to catch up with one another, learn about our respective families and careers, and make plans to get together next time he's in Denver. Similarly, I just responded to a text message to a new friend and business associate in Dubai. He inquired about when I would be able to join him for a Skype session so he could give me a virtual tour of some commercial property he's interested in developing.

These interactions aren't unique, and you probably have countless online connections and social media relationships in your personal network. Our online technology has advanced to the point where we are able to maintain a huge web of personal, professional, and public relationships with hundreds if not thousands of people around the world. What our parents would have considered science fiction, we now take for granted and use regularly as part of our everyday lives.

While technology allows us to communicate with so many people, there is a down side. In our social media-saturated, instantly "friended" world, the significance of community is frequently mentioned. Ironically enough, however, finding real connections and enduring friendships often proves challenging. For all of the many benefits of being connected across the internet, I wonder if we're losing a precious ingredient for creating lasting bonds and committed community.

BEING THERE

The commercials for tech providers—Apple, Samsung, Verizon, and many others—often emphasize the way their products allow us to stay connected with a simple call, text, Skype, chat, post or click. But here's my concern: while our ability to stay in touch with other people is greatly enhanced by technology, it's not the same thing as actually being together and sharing the important events of our lives.

It's wonderful to be able to share the live video of your child's first birthday party, but it's another to actually taste the cake, hold the little one, feel her breath blowing out the single candle, and hear her laughter in your ear as you hold her close. It's enormously beneficial and cost efficient to conduct video conferences with important clients and team members. But often you still need those face-to-face encounters to convey more than what can be read from a report or analyzed in a spreadsheet. As much as our tech-providers and online service companies want us to believe we're personally connected across the miles, it's not the same as being there.

This issue is a relatively new problem. Prior generations of Americans lived in much closer proximity, with many of them living and dying in the same vicinity as their families, friends, and peers. It's hard not to envy their sense of community and to believe it was a greater priority for most people than we place on it now. With fewer distractions on their time from technology, media, and entertainment, the majority of people enjoyed spending more time, both in quantity and in quality, together.

Today, our longing to connect and to belong remains as strong as ever; it's a fundamental part of our humanity. However, the constant fragmentation of our schedules along with the constant interruptive distraction of social media and technology makes it as challenging as it has ever been to maintain personal relationships. We've all witnessed, and likely experienced, those scenes where an entire family is together and yet each individual is looking down, glued to a phone or tablet, instead of engaging with each other.

Please understand I'm not against technology; in fact, I'm one of its biggest fans and most frequent users because of the way it allows me to conduct business on a global scale. But we have to remember that constant access does not necessarily create strong bonds. We have to make sure we stay in control of our tech devices if we want to enjoy the quality of relationships that enrich our lives and allow us to enhance the lives of others.

Today, there is tremendous pressure to work hard at all hours and constantly be "connected." At times, this constant connection to technology creates a disconnection at home. In many ways, technology has been an amazing gift for society, but like anything, it must be kept in check and used appropriately. I'm convinced there's no substitute for sitting across from a friend as he asks your advice on an issue he's facing with his kids, for sharing a meal with team members to celebrate a milestone achieved, or for shaking the hand of a new business partner.

The Fourth Ring is about investing in friendships and building community. And while technology can help you maintain relationships, it will never take the place of your personal time, attention, and interest in the people around you. The term "friend" may have evolved in today's world of virtual relationships, conversation by text, and Snapchat exchanges. But the true meaning of a good friend will never change. It's a timeless, invaluable gift as you journey through life. Without friends, there's no one to share your trials in life or to celebrate your triumphs.

ALL IN THE FAMILY

I've heard it said that "we don't get to pick our family, but we do get to pick our friends." While this is true, there's a unique bond among family members that is often the foundational glue in a person's community. In past eras, multiple generations often lived under the same roof, sharing the struggles of life as well as its joys. Some cultures still rely on this model, but here in the U.S. with our emphasis on the individual it has become harder to find. Today it may even be rare for large extended families to come together once a year at holidays or family reunions.

Beyond our spouse and our children, though, I'm convinced we need to maintain those connections to other family members as much as possible. Even small gestures like remembering shared childhood events with cousins or reaching out to send birthday or anniversary greetings can go a long way in maintaining those familial bonds. Sharing pictures of vacations and the accomplishments of our kids through an email or online message can reduce the miles. This is one of the ways we can use technology to keep up relationships that otherwise might drift.

Making the most of our extended families is rarely easy. They can sometimes frustrate us, partly because they know so much about us, and partly because we feel they may judge us or look at us as we used to be without realizing how much we've grown and changed. To our aunts and uncles, we may always be viewed as "little Bobby" or "sweet Emma," even though we're adults with successful careers and families of our own. Gentle reminders of our personal growth, such as occasional texts or calls, can sometimes help other family members see us for who we are in the present, not who we were in childhood.

Even when personality differences and personal conflicts occur, the ties that bind families together usually remain in place. I have come to learn that though family can be trying at times, there is nothing quite as rewarding as healthy family connections. You experience a deep sense of understanding, love, and acceptance as you work to cultivate and appreciate relationships with people that you didn't get to select, and can't easily ignore.

These people may often be very different from you, but I'm convinced there is a divine reason why we're put with the people in our family. Sometimes this may be for you to see what you don't want to become, but it may also be because your life and theirs will be more rich and rewarding by having experienced life together. Sharing the ups and downs of life together often forces us to draw closer to one another, despite whatever personal differences may exist among family members.

For those who have had some very trying experiences with family like I have had, I know it can be both challenging and painful. Sadly, I have experienced extended periods of time without speaking to a parent or sibling because of something they said or didn't say, something I did or didn't do. It seems that of all our relationships, those with family make us the most vulnerable, the most susceptible to pain and disappointment.

But such moments are also opportunities for personal growth, forgiveness, and healing. For those of you who can relate to such wounds, I encourage you to make amends and swallow your pride when possible, to forgive those who need forgiving and to ask forgiveness for those you may have offended, or to do whatever may be necessary to heal relationships with your family. This may not be easy, but this will allow you to be free of any contention, disappointment, or even hate that you may have for others.

Every moment you spend angry or resentful towards someone, the more control these emotions and people have over you. Free yourself by letting these people know how you truly feel, that you forgive them, and release them and yourself from these negative emotions. This does not mean you need to accept or even understand what they have done to you or others, but rather that you will become stronger and healthier through true release. Even if you feel you must separate yourself from a relationship with certain harmful family members, or they are no longer in your life, you can still forgive them—for your own sake.

DON'T WAIT UNTIL IT'S TOO LATE

I learned this lesson about forgiveness the hard way when I was sixteen years old. As I shared with you earlier, it was then that I dramatically and unexpectedly lost my beloved stepfather, Bill Watson. At that time, I was a young immortal-feeling teenager who felt he knew all he needed to know about life. But that all changed one cold January day in 1988 when Bill asked me to do some chores around the house before I left for basketball practice. Apparently, I thought it would be easier to wait and do the chores later since in my exalted opinion there was no urgency to get them done. Our different perspectives quickly escalated into one of those tense stand-offs that, looking back, seem so typical of teenagers and parents. After a heated exchange, I refused to do the chores until after basketball practice, and our lingering tension loomed like a thundercloud.

We never resolved that silly argument, and I've never been given a chance to apologize to Bill since that day.

While at basketball practice, I felt so bad about what I'd said to Bill and my overall attitude about his request that I bought him an Olathe High School Pirates t-shirt to bring home as a peace offering. Bill was very active in our local community and an avid supporter of all our local sports teams. I knew he'd like the shirt so I left it for him on the counter, knowing he'd see it when he returned that night from his business meeting in Grand Junction and hoping he'd understand the message I planned to deliver to him the next morning at breakfast.

Dog-tired from basketball practice, I went to bed early that night only to be awakened later that evening by my panicked mother. It only took me a moment to realize the source of her urgent concern. As I entered our dining room, I saw Bill bracing himself against the kitchen counter, literally gasping for air, an asthma inhaler and other medicines strewn out before him.

Apparently, Bill's insurance meeting in a client's home with pet cats had triggered a severe allergic reaction. Instead of seeking immediate medical help in Grand Junction, he decided to drive the hour home, which only allowed the allergy attack to advance even more. I quickly helped Bill to the car, and my mother sped out of the driveway to rush him to the hospital in Montrose. We lived out in the country down a gravel road, and it would be faster to drive directly to the hospital instead of waiting on an ambulance.

Shortly after I went back into the house, my mother returned with Bill. Sitting in the car constricted Bill's diaphragm, making each shallow breath even more laborious for him. So my mother had no choice but to return home and call the ambulance. By the time I carried Bill back inside, he could barely catch his breath. After what seemed like an eternity, the ambulance drove him away, while my mother and I followed in a car behind them.

On our way to the hospital in this situation, I assumed everything would be okay, that as pale and sick as Bill looked, the doctors would still "fix him" and soon he'd be home again with everything back to normal. Unfortunately for us, that was not the case. Like a scene out of a movie, I remember clearly when the doctor came into the hospital waiting room to tell us Bill had passed away from this severe asthma attack.

It was a surreal slow-motion event that did not resonate with me until my mother collapsed in my arms, tears flowing down her face. The day had started out like any other, but had ended with my life forever changed. Bill was dead and I would never have the opportunity to apologize for our argument earlier that day.

I share this story with you not for sympathy or sentimentality (although tears well up in my eyes even as I write this), but to reinforce that life is so short and our time with others fleeting and temporal. It never occurred to me that there would not be time and opportunity for me to tell Bill "I'm sorry" and "I love you" again. Though I'm sure he knew this, I didn't get the opportunity to make amends for our disagreement a few hours earlier that day. He went away healthy one afternoon, and collapsed on the floor in front of me that evening, while my "I'm sorry" gift lay upon the dining room table untouched.

None of us know how long we have to live, or how long our friends, family, or acquaintances have to live. Consequently, I encourage you to live your life so people know how you truly feel about them. You can never say "I love you" or "I care about you" too often. You can never say "I'm sorry" or "I forgive you" too soon. If you don't, you may never be given the opportunity to do so. Life can change on the proverbial dime, and in an instant you can lose what you took for granted.

Take a moment right now, and think about the people in your life. None of us are perfect—and that includes you! Is there anyone that you need to call or meet with to make amends? Make sure that people know how you feel about them by extending love, understanding, and forgiveness to them.

Don't wait on them to make the first move or start the conversation. Think about how you would feel if some tragedy occurred and you never saw this person again. What do you need to say to them? What do you need to do today, right now? Go, my friend, and make that call, send that text or email, or visit them if you can right now.

Next to your relationship with God, your spouse, and your children, the ring of family, friends, and community is a blessing, and one that you should not take for granted. Build up your community with words of encouragement, support, compassion, and forgiveness. Don't harbor grudges or allow arguments to create silent stalemates. Show your strength by letting go of old, unfinished business.

YOU'VE GOT A FRIEND

While family presents some unique challenges and benefits, our relationships with friends do as well. Friends allow us much more freedom to choose who and how we spend our time and cultivate our relationships. It is much easier to stop spending time with friends who have offended you or with whom you no longer have common interests or shared goals. But everyone longs for friends who can weather the changes of life, the kind who never feel awkward or uncertain, the kind who accept you and support you, understand and encourage you.

I suspect friendship, like true romance, can't be forced or contrived. However, just as a marriage between two people in love requires deliberate investment of time and energy in order to grow, an enduring friendship needs to be cultivated, too. The busier we become, the more we may have to make choices about which friendships we invest the most time and energy into growing. We may have to decide who we care about and with whom we want to build a deeper relationship, but there should be at least one or two friends we're always investing in no matter how busy we are.

Friends alleviate the loneliness of life by sharing their experiences and understanding and accepting the experiences you share with them. However, no one individual can meet all your emotional needs. The person who comes closest to this role should be your spouse, but even they can't be responsible for your entire mental and physical well being. Patricia is both my wife and best friend, but I know I still need other friends in order to live a healthy, balanced life.

In fact, we are each responsible for our own emotional and mental health, and often this requires that we have various friends who meet various needs. Some friendships may be more casual and limited to surface similarities such as club memberships or common interests. Some connections are for a season and based on circumstances, such as being neighbors, working on a project together at the office, or serving together on a committee or board. Other friendships will run deeper and involve shared dreams and connections on more than one level. These friends "get" you and you instinctively trust them and want to be there for them.

Finally, there are a handful of friends that you may be fortunate to sustain over your lifetime. These may require more effort in terms of deliberate communication and visits with one another, but these friendships are often the most rewarding. Having someone who has known you through decades of your life creates a bond so familiar and special. They have seen you grow, change, endure, suffer, overcome, and thrive and been in your corner the whole time.

If I'm honest, it's probably more difficult for me to sustain my friendships now than ever before. With a beautiful wife, an adult daughter, and two active teenaged boys, and my business growing in leaps and bounds, I have to be careful how I invest my time. Obviously, Patricia and our children take priority. But I've learned that the busier and more hectic my life becomes, the more I need a few good friends. Otherwise, it's too easy to isolate myself and become distracted by work and other "urgent" responsibilities.

It's almost unheard of in our nanosecond culture, but I think it's more important than ever to go fishing with buddies or to catch a Broncos or Nuggets game when we can. As friends we can remind each other of our true priorities and challenge each other without trying to compete (unless we're on the basketball court) to be better men. So often in our culture men especially are told we should be loners, self-sufficient, unemotional and independent.

However, the truth is that no matter how successful we may be, or how busy we may be, we still need friends. Someone who is rooting for us no matter what. Who cares about the state of our marriage and knows what grade our kids are in. Someone whose presence enhances our life in immeasurable ways. Someone who will speak truth into our lives, hold us accountable, and be there in the worst of times.

Someone who models the kind of friend we want to be.

WHERE YOU BELONG

I fear we have lost a deep understanding of what community means in our American society. If you think I'm romanticizing the past or being nostalgic, stop and think about how many of your neighbors you currently know. Not just their names, but ones you have actually met and taken the time to get to know a little.

Do you know the people next door, three doors down, or those a couple blocks away? What about the people in your local church, or in the nearby senior living center, or in the cancer ward at the nearest hospital? These people are all part of our "community," or at least they should be. In our rush to be successful, independent, and self-sufficient, we seem to have lost a sense of connection to other people and their welfare. If others don't directly intersect or impact our lives, we fail to pursue them or to serve them, missing out on the richness they would add to our lives.

There's really only one remedy for strengthening these relationships. Each of us needs to consider our definition of "community" and to expand it beyond our street, our race, our economic status, and our comfort zone. This creates an opportunity to learn and grow from others, especially those that may be different from us. Although you may think these people are radically different than you and your "tribe," when you give them a chance and get to know them, you will discover you have many of the important things in common with them. As humans we all share the pursuit of happiness, the will to survive and make a difference, and the desire to be known, liked, and loved. We all want to belong.

Think about someone to whom you can reach out and begin to build an authentic and meaningful relationship. What is stopping you from doing this? Be bold, be courageous, be the friend that you would like to have in your own life. Make the call. Send the email. Drive to their neighborhood. Share a cup of coffee. Take an hour to focus on someone other than yourself and those in your immediate relational circle.

Community is important as it is part of the rich fabric of life. By getting to know our neighbors, and people in our town or city, we develop relationships of understanding and support. Granted we are all busy and are at times just trying to survive ourselves, but don't lose out on the opportunity to say hello, to invite people over for a meal, or to go into another neighborhood to serve. You will be glad that you did so, and they will be grateful for your caring.

We all want to enjoy our lives, but so often we fail to prioritize the elements that can enrich us the most. Building a diverse community of family, friends, neighbors, and others around you will enhance your life more than you realize. It's worth the time, effort, and trouble. Make the Fourth Ring of your life a priority before it's too late and you realize you've missed out on one of life's greatest joys: a simple, yet profound connection to another human being.

RING OF TRUTH
7 QUOTATIONS TO CONSIDER

"One can acquire everything in solitude except character." | **Stendhal**

"No man is an island, entire of itself; every man is a piece of the continent, a part of the main. If a clod be washed away by the sea, Europe is the less, as well as if a promontory were, as well as if a manor of thy friend's or of thine own were: any man's death diminishes me, because I am involved in mankind, and therefore never send to know for whom the bells tolls; it tolls for thee." | **John Donne**

"Strength lies in differences, not in similarities." | **Stephen R. Covey**

"If man is to survive, he will have learned to take a delight in the essential differences between men and between cultures. He will learn that differences in ideas and attitudes are a delight, part of life's exciting variety, not something to fear." | **Gene Roddenberry**

"You don't choose your family. They are God's gift to you, as you are to them." | **Desmond Tutu**

"The love of family and the admiration of friends is much more important than wealth and privilege." | **Charles Kuralt**

"In every conceivable manner, the family is link to our past, bridge to our future." | **Alex Haley**

RING OF HONOR
QUESTIONS FOR REFLECTION

How are your relationships with your family, truly? Do you need to reach out to someone and have an open, honest conversation about something between you? Do they know how you truly feel about them?

_____

_____

_____

_____

_____

Is there someone in your life that you need to forgive, or do you need forgiveness from someone? What is stopping you from doing this today? Is your pride worth losing the opportunity to have peace between you?

_____

_____

_____

_____

Do you have authentic quality relationships in your life? If not, what is stopping you from making these friendships flourish?

_____

_____

_____

_____

Are you the friend that you wish you had? How can you be a better friend, family member, and community member?

_____

_____

_____

_____

_____

How do you define "community"? Write out your definition in one sentence. Can you expand this definition to include more people that look, think, and come from different backgrounds than you?

_____

_____

_____

_____

_____

CHAPTER 6

THE FIFTH RING:
FOR THE LOVE OF COUNTRY

"I like to see a man proud of the place in which he lives. I like to see a man live so that his place will be proud of him." | **Abraham Lincoln**

I have been fortunate to experience many other places and cultures throughout a good part of the world. As you may recall, I had planned to serve in the Peace Corps right out of college until the discovery of an allergic reaction to a childhood bee sting derailed my qualification under the Corps' stringent health standards. But that disappointment has faded over time as I've traveled to so many amazing and unique locales, sometimes for vacation but often for business and service opportunities.

A large amount of this travel has occurred south of the equator in countries often referred to as "third world," although I've never particularly liked that term or its implications. I have also visited Europe and many countries above the equator as well. While I appreciate, respect, and enjoy my visits around the globe, they always remind me "there's no place like home."

Such travel has provided me with a better understanding and appreciation of other cultures and people, while also doing the same for my own country. In fact, I have developed an even deeper love for America by visiting and engaging with the people of other countries. I've become convinced you sometimes have to step out of your own culture in order to have a better understanding and appreciation for it.

THIS LAND IS MY LAND

No matter how fascinated I have been by the native cultures in Brazil, Kenya, India, China, Europe, or the Middle East, I have never encountered a country or a people quite like that of the United States of America. Clearly part of this affinity is biased, given that I am a proud American citizen and patriot, but it goes much deeper than this. As someone who has studied world history and politics, I have come to understand that the United States is a very special place indeed. There is literally no place like it in the world.

This uniqueness began with our very founding as a country, from the time that people risked everything to pursue settling a new land and on through the writing of The Declaration of Independence and our Constitution. These latter two milestones remain unique and awe-inspiring documents that promote the concept of individual rights, equality of all people, and our freedom as a people to govern ourselves through a Constitutional Republic. Never before, not even in ancient Greece and Rome, had such radical ideas been put forth, by leaders who would normally seize power for themselves versus realizing it should be with the people all along. This concept cannot be trivialized, for it has transformed the people we call Americans and the entire world forever.

Before exploring these ideas further, I want to expand upon the concept of a Constitutional Republic. Most Americans believe we live in a Democracy, but this is not true. Instead, our Founding Fathers created a system that is governed by a Constitution, a truly profound document that we will explore in more detail later. The Founders knew we needed a republic that would allow for the people to elect representatives who would carry their interests into the halls of government, representatives who would truly represent the interests of the people, not themselves.

Consequently, we are not a pure democracy, as we do not vote on every single issue. Rather, our representatives use the framework of the Constitution to protect the rights of the people from governmental control and develop legislation to ensure the protection of those rights. Sadly, we have transitioned into believing the role of government is to take care of all the ills in society, and that since government leaders must know best, they should control the people, rather than the people having control of their own destinies and free will.

Today, some people view the Founding Fathers as "racist" or "hypocrites" because they wrote words that spoke of freedom for all, yet all people were not given freedom at the founding of our country. Though our Founding Fathers were imperfect, just as we are today, they wrote divinely inspired documents that aspired to ideals above themselves. Yes, they were human, with their own faults, scars, and weaknesses, but the Declaration of Independence and the Constitution, and the system of government that they helped to put into place, were both timeless and progressive.

I'm convinced our Founders knew future generations of their new republic would develop and aspire to achieve greatness over time. Therefore, the ideas they put forth allowed Americans to aspire to this greatness, to break free from their bonds of historical patronage, and to embody a spirit of freedom, individualism, and equality. No, those

Founders were not perfect, but somehow they came together to draft near-perfect documents that continue to endure over two centuries later, and for their great efforts we should celebrate and honor them.

WINNING HISTORY'S LOTTERY

Just imagine if our current political leaders were tasked with writing a Declaration of Independence or a Constitution that would help launch and empower a country. Do you think they could actually get this done, given all of their bickering, self-centered motives, and short-sighted decisions? Sadly, I do not believe they could, as today we can rarely get a balanced budget passed. At times, I believe our Founding Fathers would weep to see what our country has become. In many ways we have attained greatness, and in some ways we have fallen short of the true potential that they envisioned and for which they sacrificed so much.

Though we have our challenges as a country, just as any nation does, I'm convinced we have won the historical lottery of all time: to live where, and when, and how we do in the United States of America today. The majority of our population truly lives better than kings and queens of antiquity. Regardless of income level, today most of us enjoy not only access to basics such as food, shelter, and employment, but also opportunities for improving our education, our jobs, and our leisure time.

Before you dismiss my claim as hyperbole, I encourage you to compare the average life expectancy of an American to the ancient Pharaohs of Egypt, or our ability to access food in mass to someone trying to survive in the 1100s. Go to a neighborhood grocery store and consider the amazing quantity and diversity of food choices, including fresh fruits and vegetables from all around the world, regardless of the time of year. Royalty from ancient times never had so much choice, access, leisure time, and quality of life. True, not all members of our society are living an easy, well-fed or well-sheltered life, but the vast majority of our citizens in the U.S. have access and opportunities available to them that the majority of humanity throughout world history never experienced or thought possible.

The United States is unique in that it empowers people with inalienable rights and a free system of opportunity to live in. These rights do not come from our government or other people, but rather these are Natural Rights provided by our Creator. They allow humans to soar to their greatest potential and to pursue their dreams. One's history, background, and family name do not matter as much as their ambition, initiative, hard work, and effort to make something better of themselves. Our national environment allows for creativity, rewards, and consequences that create an atmosphere of immense productivity. This attitude toward the rights of an individual is contagious and remains one of the main reasons we have helped to transform the world for the better.

For one moment, imagine that the United States of America has never existed. This includes every invention, every thought, every law, and everything else that has been created in America. It simply does not exist, or at least was not created by this country. What type of world would we have?

I suspect we would have a world very similar to the dawn of the Industrial Revolution, a world where one's family name or history take precedence over one's own will, hard work, and personal contributions. A world of fewer "haves" and more "have nots." A world where power, lineage, and money would further silence and control the less fortunate. A world where human rights and dignity are bestowed upon a few only if they are in favor of those in power. We can only imagine, but I firmly believe we would have a much darker, less developed environment that does not provide nearly as much opportunity for as many individuals throughout the world as we do now.

To be clear, I am not stating that the United States is perfect, that we have only done good things in the world, or that all people are perfectly well off. What I am stating is that by and large, we have had an amazingly positive and transformational impact in the world, and that the world is a better place because of what our ancestors ignited. For this reason, protecting, supporting, and developing our country is my Sixth Ring.

KNOWLEDGE IS POWER

I've heard it said, "If you take something for granted, it will be taken away from you." This adage certainly holds true for our country. We have a responsibility that has been handed down from the Founding Fathers, a charge to protect and uphold this great experiment in government: our Constitutional Republic. We do this by being informed, not just by sound bites from a potentially biased news source, but through reading, seeking knowledge, and communicating with our neighbors.

Through these actions we become engaged. Engaged to vote, engaged to hold our representatives and government accountable, and engaged to leave this great country in a better state for the next generation. If we truly commit to this as a people, it would be positively transformational. If not, then we risk jeopardizing the very freedoms that are often taken for granted. We must remember the wise observation made by U.S. President Ronald Reagan: "Freedom is never more than one generation away from extinction. We didn't pass it to our children in the bloodstream. It must be fought for, protected, and handed on for them to do the same, or one day we will spend our sunset years telling our children and our children's children what it was once like in the United States where men were free."

So what does this responsibility look like in practice? First of all, achieving and maintaining a basic education—math, reading, writing, history, and science—provides the foundation for becoming an engaged citizen and actively participating in government. Without this basic understanding of the world, we're sorely limited in the ability to have informed opinions about the issues of life. Knowledge is indeed power, and each person should be empowered by securing basic knowledge for themselves.

Second, this educational foundation enables one to achieve their dreams, whether that be launching a business, patenting new inventions, serving the community, writing books, or anything else they dream for themselves. Such work and service leads to the enrichment of our communities, our culture, and our country in general. Without each person contributing in some way, it lessens the overall atmosphere for all of us. By having an educated and informed populace engaged in creating a positive difference in some way, we can then vote for representatives in our society more effectively.

This latter point is vitally important, as voting for the best people to help represent us in government is one of the most effective ways to ensure our great society remains strong. If you are not voting, then I don't think you should be complaining about issues or problems in our country. It's always easier to play armchair quarterback and sideline critic than to participate actively toward positive change. Voting is a powerful tool, and you have been given the awesome opportunity of participating in this process. Please don't take this civic duty for granted.

ACTIVE PARTICIPATION

There's another old saying that holds true with politics: "we get what we deserve." If you are disgusted with the type of people in politics, the graft and dishonesty in the system, or the government attempting to limit your freedoms, then you must be a catalyst for change. Otherwise, we get exactly what we deserve as citizens who are not taking an active role in supporting and voting for the people who will actually make a positive change. Vote!

At times I meet people who state politely that they're "not political" or "not into politics." When I hear this, I ask them a few simple questions:

Are you alive? Do you have a family, a job, or a place to live? Do you eat, breathe, or travel? If you do any of these activities, you are involved in politics whether you want to be or not! The only question that remains is whether you have any say in the process. Politics will always have an effect on you, but will you exercise the privilege you have effecting change in politics?

Do you believe our Founding Fathers and all the people who shed blood for our country during the past two hundred years sacrificed so much so you could have a mediocre life ignoring your government? Do you believe they envisioned a future where big government programs would grow so big that they have limited your freedom, mortgaged your future, and are now demanding most of your hard work, ideas, and resources in the form of taxes to them? Since when did we abdicate our responsibility to carry the torch of true Freedom and Liberty high and instead assume that big government had a right to do to us whatever it chooses?

Ask yourself this question honestly: What is the true role of government as defined by our Founding Fathers? Is our current government really honoring the powers that we gave them, or have they taken more and more from us in the form of laws, the establishment of bureaus and all types of programs? If you are 100% happy with the job that big government is doing, then I suppose you can do nothing in good conscience. If, however, you are concerned, fed up, or disheartened with what is happening in our schools, communities, and country, then I encourage you to get informed and get involved. Single individuals and small bands of people have helped to transform the world at times, and you may be that very person who is called to make the change you long to see.

The amazing thing is that the foundational pillars of our country still allow you to have this impact, but you must act without delay. Think for a moment what it would be like for you leave your mark, your fingerprint upon society. This can be done by voting with your heart and mind instead of relying by default on your chosen political party. Change can be accomplished by starting a petition, writing a blog, getting involved in a political campaign of someone you believe in, running for office yourself, and in many more ways.

Remember, people who want power for themselves want you to be uninformed, apathetic, and just "comfortable enough" so you won't take action and challenge them. By having you off the field of the competition of ideas, they can have complete control. We cannot be frogs in the proverbial pot of boiling water, just sitting there content until we are boiled alive. Each of us has a role to play, and each of us must take the field to ensure that our country endures. Anything less would be a disservice to all who have given so much to make the United States of America so great.

RUNNING FOR OFFICE

Feeling privileged by such a responsibility, I try to contribute my part, which is my Sixth Ring, as it affects all of the prior rings I hold dear in my life. For my family, this means getting involved in campaigns, issues, and hosting informational events at our home. Whether this is for politics, non-profits, or people with good hearts and great ideas, we try to take the public square and recreate it in our living room. Whether people agree or disagree with a particular speaker, cause, or idea, it is important that they are informed and given the chance to ask the tough questions so they can make their decisions properly.

In addition to hosting events, I decided a few years ago to found The Opportunity Coalition (www.opportunitycoalition.com). The idea for this organization took root soon after I ran for the Colorado State House of Representatives, HD-3, for the 2012 election year. Since I was a young boy, I have always been drawn to the idea of serving our country through public office. I'm unsure where this calling came from, but I have always admired people who have served their country in this way, especially those who truly made a positive difference to impact the world for the better.

These people are very rare, the ones who remain selfless and truly strive to make a difference, versus those involved in "politics" who are only trying to manipulate the system for their own personal benefit. We need true statesmen who care about the next generation, and fewer politicians who only care about themselves.

My race for public office was considered one of the top-contested races in the State of Colorado, and my team and I were also told that it was one of the top fifty races in the country identified by the opposition as one they would like to win. I ran as a first-time candidate during the year that Mitt Romney was running against President Barrack Obama. My opponent was a multi-term incumbent, who was originally from England. This individual was the opposite of someone like me, as he was from a wealthy English family, was an attorney by trade, and believed that the government should control the lives of people instead of allowing people more freedom to live their lives. Determined to fill a critical role, I launched a fresh and positive campaign to unseat this career politician.

Though we raised more money than any State House candidate had ever raised prior or since in the State of Colorado, and though we knocked on many more doors than our opponent and attended many more community events connecting with the people of the District, the opposition found a strategy for attacking my character. My opponent's team launched a negative and untrue campaign against me by stating that I owed $269,000 in back taxes to the IRS.

Though this claim was false, and though we provided letters from my CPA and attorney that disproved these statements, the opposition continued to flood people's mailboxes with negative ad after negative ad, all focusing on this false accusation. Although I pay a tremendous amount in taxes, including property taxes in the 17 states where we own commercial real estate assets, leave it to big government bureaucrats to come up with a lie about taxes. They would not focus on the issues, nor would they rescind their statements, even though we were open and transparent with the public.

On Election Day, the opposition even hired an airplane that flew around the District carrying a banner that read: "Brian Watson, pay your taxes!" Unfortunately, we lost that race, but it remains one of the best experiences of my life. True, I did not like losing the race, but I thoroughly enjoyed walking neighborhoods every day, meeting people, discussing ideas, giving talks about issues in public, and working with an amazing group of campaign volunteers who remain good friends to this day. Raising financial support was also something I enjoyed, as I have had to "dial for dollars" ever since I started in business at Cushman & Wakefield of Colorado.

The morning after election night, I was back in my office at Northstar Commercial Partners by 6:30 a.m., working. I have never been the type of person to give up, or to stay down long after having the wind knocked out of me. I think this comes from when I was young. Whenever I got bucked off a horse I'd been riding, my parents would tell me to dust myself off and get back on as soon as I could. They said if I didn't, I'd develop a fear of horses and riding, which was simply unacceptable. While I suspect my opponent's supporters hoped I might disappear after the campaign, my loss only emboldened me to get more involved, and to try and make a positive difference in every way I can. Whether I held an office or not, I remained committed to making a positive impact for as many people as I could. This is when I started brainstorming ways to unite people and create opportunities for positive change, which birthed the Opportunity Coalition.

OPPORTUNITY FOR GREATNESS

You see, while running for office, I noticed that people were somewhat disconnected in the State of Colorado. There were people from the Western Slope where I grew up, Mountain areas, Front Range, and Eastern Plains. Given the differences in their local communities, many of these people did not "connect" with each other on their respective regional concerns and issues. In addition, there were people who were mainly focused on being connected to those in their particular industry, or in their particular arena of politics, education, legal, non-profit work, etc. As someone who loves people, loves the great State of Colorado, and who likes bringing good people together to create more opportunity for all, I decided to create the Opportunity Coalition (www.opportunitycoalition.com).

The purpose of the Opportunity Coalition is to promote the ideals of free enterprise, entrepreneurship, and freedom by connecting people throughout the State of Colorado. We believe that by bringing good people together in a positive atmosphere that works to break down barriers, we will create "bridges of connection" and "sparks of collaboration" that will make our great State even better. Each month, we host a speaker who has been influential and successful in some way.

Our events are usually held at the Innovation Pavilion, an 85,000 square foot office building that my company Northstar Commercial Partners acquired as a distressed asset from a lender through one of our partnerships. The Innovation Pavilion is one of the most successful business incubators in our State. It has helped over 80 companies start or grow in this unique entrepreneurial community, and its entrepreneurs range in age from the age of 10 to over 75.

We bought the mostly vacant building and improved the space to help these companies grow and empower its occupants to achieve great success in their pursuit of the American Dream. Consequently, we thought that this would be the perfect environment to host the Opportunity Coalition's monthly speaker series, as each guest speaker gives a talk about their history, company, and/or initiative that has made a positive difference. They may come from various backgrounds in business, law, non-profits, medical, academia, government, or a host of other professions, but they all share a desire to share what they have learned, to empower people, and to make Colorado a better place.

Through these events, people have started new companies and initiatives together, new employees and partners have been found, new business has been secured, and people have learned from our speakers and the other guests. We welcome everyone because we believe "high tides raise all boats," and our job is to create an environment where diverse people are respected, encouraged, and rewarded for their creative ideas and hard work. This is the American Dream in action, with human faces and community-driven hearts, and we are humbled to have a small part in helping to make this connection happen for many.

In addition to the monthly speaker series at the Innovation Pavilion, I also created an Opportunity Coalition Podcast. In these interviews, I speak with one or two influential and successful people from various sectors throughout America. These are unique people with wonderful and interesting stories to share. Through a casual phone conversation we discuss their company, initiative, or cause, and their personal history. Each of these podcasts lasts 30-40 minutes, and allows subscribers to listen to these interviews on the way to work, at home, while working out, or at any other convenient time.

These are listed for free on iTunes or at www.opportunitycoalition.com, and anyone can listen and learn about an interesting business, topic, individual, or initiative. This in turn may spark new ideas, encouragement, and greater knowledge to achieve their personal goals. I have been blessed in meeting many interesting people from the U.S. and throughout the world, and I like to share these experiences and relationships with others.

We hope that we have contributed some part in making our State of Colorado better, our great U.S.A. stronger, and our world a more enjoyable, cleaner, and safer place that provides opportunity and empowerment for *all* people. By no means have we helped solve all the problems that may exist, but just maybe, we have helped improve at least one person's life for the better. As my parents often said, try to help as many as you can, but focus on the one first.

We can help so many people in our country and world by doing our part to make America the best that it can be. It starts with each of us taking the responsibility to do our part. Our great nation still shines as a beacon of hope that draws many from around the world. This is partly due to some profound ideas and documents that were established at the founding of our country and some amazing people we call Americans today, who have helped to transform our world for the better. Please join me in the quest to sustain and build freedom and opportunity for all American citizens, so we may continue to be that bright beacon upon the hill, illuminating the darkness.

RING OF TRUTH
7 QUOTATIONS TO CONSIDER

"You and I have a rendezvous with destiny. We will preserve for our children this, the last best hope of man on earth, or we will sentence them to take the first step into a thousand years of darkness. If we fail, at least let our children and our children's children say of us we justified our brief moment here. We did all that could be done." | **Ronald Reagan**

"History has taught us over and over again that freedom is not free. When push comes to shove, the ultimate protectors of freedom and liberty are the brave men and women in our armed forces. Throughout our history, they've answered the call in bravery and sacrifice." | **Tim Pawlenty**

"We can't all be Washingtons, but we can all be patriots." | **Charles F. Browne**

"The cement of this union is the heart-blood of every American." | **Thomas Jefferson**

"America is much more than a geographical fact. It is a political and moral fact—the first community in which men set out in principle to institutionalize freedom, responsible government, and human equality." | **Adlai Stevenson**

"Where liberty dwells, there is my country." | **Benjamin Franklin**

"Freedom lies in being bold." | **Robert Frost**

RING OF HONOR
QUESTIONS FOR REFLECTION

List at least five qualities of our country that make you proud to be an American. Which of these do you believe to be most important for making us such a great nation? Why?

_____

_____

_____

_____

_____

_____

_____

What do you believe is the greatest threat or challenging issue facing America today? What can you do about this—starting right now, today—to make it better?

_____

_____

_____

_____

_____

_____

_____

If you could make one change in the world that would help transform the quality of life and opportunity for many people, what would that change be? What prevents you from starting the process that can bring this change to life?

_____

_____

_____

_____

_____

Considering your own personal talents, abilities, and resources, how can you best serve your country and fellow human beings?

_____

_____

_____

_____

_____

Are you politically informed and active about issues facing your neighborhood? Your county or state district? Your state and region of the country? About our nation? And the rest of the world? Name at least three actions you can take to increase your knowledge and participation in solving problems and pursuing opportunities for growth in at least two of these areas.

_____

_____

_____

_____

_____

CHAPTER 7

THE SIXTH RING:
YOUR PLACE IN THE WORLD

"The best way to find yourself is to lose yourself in the service of others." | **Mahatma Gandhi**

One of the great blessings we have in life is to serve our fellow human beings. Such service—motivated by compassion and fueled by love—not only reminds us of our connections to others, but also reinforces our stewardship of our environment and the world we live in. Some people believe serving the needs of others and environmental conservation are mutually exclusive and in conflict with each other. However, I would submit the exact opposite is true; you can't serve your fellow human beings effectively if you don't have a healthy environment from which to serve.

If you don't have a model for how to serve your fellow human beings and the environment, you will need to develop your own resourceful methods. In my experience, the hardest part is often putting the needs of others alongside or above your own, seeing the world through their eyes and not just your own individual perspective. Unfortunately, this is often easier said than done.

Humans by nature can be self-centered and focused on our own survival, success, and happiness before those of others. This is the main reason people often use the term "human nature" in a base context because, when left to our own devices and desires, we will focus on our ourselves and our own well-being ahead of those around us. We usually have to be trained and motivated to rank others' needs as equal to our own—let alone to put their needs *ahead* of our own.

My Sixth Ring is how you relate to the rest of the world, both the people and the planet. I'm convinced in order to know how to serve others and to be a good steward of all the resources entrusted to you, a person must recognize how they fit in the world, their unique place and purpose, where they belong and what they were made to do. Once you discover this aspect of yourself, then the way you relate to the world will never be the same.

SURVIVAL OF THE FITTEST

Maybe you're thinking, "It's natural to put our own needs and desires first. It's just the way people are." Certainly, such self-preoccupation and self-preservation are the norm for almost all living organisms. But humans are not just any "organism." We are a unique and complex species that has been given the highest performing brain, the ability of self-actualization, and an eternal soul.

Perhaps you don't often think of yourself in this context or marvel at the uniqueness of a human life and its many facets. Find the nearest mirror and take a moment to look at yourself. Seriously, look at yourself for at least sixty seconds. You may have become conditioned by our culture to focus on your flaws or wrinkles and overlook the extraordinary life form gazing back at you. But look past what you may not like about yourself and your appearance. Go beyond what you can see on the surface. Instead focus on the intricacies of your body, the special, individualized memories stored in your brain, or the way a child's laugh delights your soul.

You are a one-of-a-kind creation, unlike any other animal or human being on the planet. There has never been anyone exactly like you, nor will there ever be in all of time. *Ever.* Let this truly sink in for a few minutes. Please don't take this for granted or dismiss it as something you've heard before. If you need more help or incentive, just think for a moment of how celebrated you would be if you were the first life-form that we discovered on another planet. Discovering such a dynamic creature would be miraculous—and so are you.

Now contrast this truth with the belief that humans are just a random collision of molecules and amoebas that came together to create more complex organisms that eventually became the human being. But consider the logic of this idea of evolving progression. I once heard the likelihood of human beings developing this way to be about the same as if a series of tornadoes blew through a junkyard over millions of years until eventually a brand new fully loaded Ferrari emerged from the accumulation of random parts. Though a species may change over time in what's known as adaptation, it takes a very large stretch of the imagination to believe humans evolved from single-celled sea life.

SQUARE PEGS AND ROUND SOULS

I've always thought that we humans don't belong here on earth—we're just not suited for it. Consider, for instance, that we're the only organism that walks upright, exposing its most vital organs to potential threats ahead of us. Our skin isn't thick and doesn't harden into a leathery shell. We don't have enough hair, claws, or teeth to protect us from nature.

We are the only creature that creates artificial environments, controls temperature to meet our desires, and builds and destroys environments at our will. The rest of the animal kingdom works in concert with each other, but we dominate, destroy, and create all upon our will. We do not belong here, we are in conflict with our environment, and we should not survive by the laws of Nature, and thus I believe we are made in the image of our divine Creator.

Another piece of evidence supporting this conclusion comes from the way people seek meaning in their lives. The question "what is my purpose?" looms large for virtually all people across history and most civilized cultures. Especially when other primary needs such as food, water, and shelter are met, human beings endeavor to create a life that is productive and fulfilling. We want our existence to matter in a way that transcends our everyday lives of eating, sleeping, and working.

The concept of questioning one's purpose is not easily resolved for most people. Often we must experience failure, fear, and frustration before we're willing to take a risk and make a change to improve our lives. We ask this question because we know inside that we were "meant for something more." All of us have this. It is part of being alive and conscious of our mortality. Numerous doctors and neurologists have concluded human beings are hardwired for fulfillment.

Unfortunately, this desire can lead some people down dark and destructive roads. In an effort to seek out and fulfill this human need for purpose, we can easily fill our lives with "stuff" to abate the desire. This "stuff" not only comes in the form of material possessions. Anything that consumes us, drives us, pacifies us can easily become the false center of our lives. As a result, we then struggle with addictions, co-dependencies, exploitation of others, and various religious beliefs or doctrines that meet our temporary and subjective needs.

Many ancient philosophers, scientists, and theologians have concluded that humans can only address this desire by spiritual means. The most compelling source for me is the Bible, which also confirms that a void exists within us. This spiritual longing motivates us to define and to exercise our purpose. Consequently, when we understand this divine purpose, we can fill the void within ourselves by allowing it to lead us to God. You see, the Bible describes this emptiness within us as a desire to know God. We are made in his image and long to reconnect with the Creator who designed us from the inside out. Therefore, only one solution will lead to true, lasting satisfaction.

If you do not fill this void with its rightful occupant, you will never be truly fulfilled. For example, if you use the proverbial "trying to fit a square peg into a round hole," either one of two things will happen. Either the peg will not fit into the hole because it was not designed to fit there, or else the square peg, being much smaller than the round hole, will fit very loosely, never fitting completely and wholly.

The application of this maxim to our human desire for purpose is that you need to fill the God-shaped void with God. If you try to put material possessions in this void it will either not fit, or fit loosely in an unstable basis. This is why you see people jump from one "filler" to the next, just searching for something to pour into the void. But this only results in more frustration and desperation.

The solution is both simple and yet complex. I suspect God intends for our need for him to be quite clear and self-evident, but people find ways of avoiding such straightforward truth in order to maintain the illusion of control over their lives. It's the tension we see between the way so many people consider themselves "spiritual" but not "religious." They know there's more to life than what we see on the surface, thus their acknowledgement of the spiritual. Yet they are repelled by the human agendas—personally, socially, politically, and more—in most traditional faith systems and organized religions.

VERDICT OF TRUTH

If you consider yourself in this camp, I recommend putting your concerns about religion aside for a moment and focusing on what you really know and believe about God. The Lord gave each of us a large God-shaped void because he wants to be a big part of our lives. If the void wasn't large enough, we would never be hungry enough to seek him. Consequently, you may be missing out on leading the tremendous life God created you to have. You may be dissatisfied, disappointed, and discouraged because you're filling your life with possessions, achievements, or relationships with others. These are all gifts from God to be enjoyed, but no object, person, or accomplishment can fill your soul the way a relationship with God can.

God desires us, his creation, to be tethered to him. Such fullness in the divine leads to a life of contentment, service, happiness, truth, strength and love. The Lord knows you have this longing to understand your purpose here on this earth. He put it within you! Given that he created this place inside you, it is up to you to seek him in order to discover all he has for you.

If you don't believe this, let me be the first to challenge you to reconsider your assumptions. Because here's the truth: **You are a uniquely created**

being, made by a God who loves you and desires that you be in a relationship with him. Be honest with yourself and reflect on this bold statement for a moment.

Maybe you're asking, "But, Brian, how do you *know* this is true?" There are many people who make grand and bold statements, but can they back them up? Please allow me this opportunity to share with you the basis for my own personal faith and belief in a divine Creator. In order to verify my assertion, I need to break it down into its components and verify each of them. So let's consider them one proposition at a time.

1) You are a uniquely created being.

Look around you right now. What do you see? Are there other people nearby? Is there land or water? Do you see trees and plants, clouds in the sky? What animals are near?

My guess is that wherever you are reading this now, there is life. This may take the form of various biospheres, but either way there is a representation of life. Do you notice anything in particular? Does anything look out of place? Do you feel like you belong in the setting where you find yourself right now? Why or why not? In looking at yourself and the earth as a whole, there is one organism that is in total contrast to its environment: the human being.

We should never have existed as long as we have. And yet here we are, thriving with new life and new advancements. I recall in college anthropology classes we studied the evolution theories. As an avid reader, I've perused many additional scientific articles and books over the years since then. After reading all of this material, I am still caught on Chapter VIII of Darwin's *The Origin of Species*. In this chapter Darwin examines the problem that sterility of hybrid species poses to his hypothesis of natural selection as well as the lack of evidence during the time intervals required for evolution to occur. I'm no scientist, but basically, Darwin comes up lacking and questioning his entire theory in Chapter VIII. The scientist whose name has become synonymous with evolution still doubted his own theories!

No matter what the study, do you ever just scratch your head wondering why *homo sapiens* are so different from the world around them? Do you really believe that some microscopic organisms came together on a completely random basis to form humans? Do you really believe the miracle that is your life—body, mind, spirit—just came together by accident or by random collision of molecules? Could DaVinci or Rembrandt have created their works of art by blindfolding themselves and throwing paint at their canvases?

This doesn't even take into account all of the various miraculous parts of our bodies and their various systems: nervous, muscular, neurological, cardiac, pulmonary, on and on. Most of us would agree with adaptation, the evolution within species, that occurs over time and is often influenced by environmental factors. However, pure evolution from nothingness into masterful greatness is a bigger leap of faith than to consider divine intervention!

Unless you have an identical twin, my guess is that you have never met anyone that looks or acts exactly like you. That is because you were uniquely made. There is only one of you on this planet, and that will be the only one to ever exist. Ever. Humans were placed here by a divine Creator. What else can explain why we are in such contrast to our environment, or why we have succeeded despite our frail conditions?

2) You were created by God.

The Bible states that God created the heavens, the earth, and life itself— the divine "Big Bang" theory! Suddenly, God decided to create life, which led to his decision to create humans so he could be in relationship with them. The reason we are in stark contrast to our worldly environment is that God created us in his image. You have been uniquely chosen and created by the Creator of the Universe. Your life is no random event or accident. You are a one-of-a-kind designer original!

3) *God is for you.*

Have you ever heard that "God loves you"? It may sound trite or even flattering, but what does it really mean—assuming that it's even true? First, the Bible tells us that God is the origin and source of all love. The very concept of love comes as a gift from our Creator. This type of unconditional, compassionate, gracious love transcends our human notions of love. The Greek word for this special kind of love is *agape*, a never-ending, self-sacrificing, fully-accepting love. It is for everyone, forever.

Perhaps the greatest evidence for God's love is his limitless grace. In fact, from my studies of various faiths and belief systems, I've learned divine grace is a uniquely Christian concept. Unlike other faiths in which you must work through your sin or life's condition, God freely gives us grace. We need his grace because he also gave us free will to choose how we live. He wanted us to accept his love and follow his guidance in response to his love, not because he forced us to comply.

However, it's no surprise that humans originally decided to turn away from God in their use of free will. This separation from God is a word that's become very "religious" and emotionally charged for most people: sin. Originally the word "sin" meant "missing the mark," the way a shooter misses hitting the target. Humans are perfectly flawed but God is perfectly holy. In order to close this gap between us, God performed his biggest act of love, by allowing His son Jesus to come to earth in human form.

Jesus gave us a firsthand example of how to practice love during His time on earth. These lessons are explained in the New Testament of the Bible. His final act of love in human form was to die on the cross as the perfect sacrifice for our sins. By this act, Jesus took away our sin so we can be rejoined in God's presence upon our death. In taking a perfect sinless being in the form of Jesus and giving him as a sacrifice, the rest of us sin-filled humans can be rejoined in the presence of God's holy perfection.

But there is a catch: this can only occur if we recognize and accept Jesus's act on the cross and acknowledge him as our Lord and Savior. It is very clear that God loves you and desperately wants you, his beloved creation, to be rejoined with him for eternity. Otherwise, why would he give up his only Son?

4) God wants a close relationship with you.

As you can see, you're already in a relationship with God even if you do not want to be. You are part of a divine epic, an eternal story filled with conflicts, temptations, trials, sacrifices, and celebrations. There are battles against a spiritual enemy who wants to separate you from God and consume you and derail your special purpose in life.

You may choose not to acknowledge or participate in this drama, but that does not change the fact that you are encompassed within it. True, you may be off center stage preoccupied with some facet of your life, trying to look busy, or choosing to ignore the larger context of the truth around you. But whatever the case, you are still here, alive on this planet right now at this time.

The question is this: will you enter into a relationship with the director of life or will you shrink into the shadows hoping that no one will recognize you? Rather than mediocrity and desolation, why don't you try moving into the light? God is waiting there for you, waiting to embrace you and satisfy the spiritual hunger deep within. A life in the Lord is rich in blessings, and all you have to do is acknowledge and accept him into your life.

The choice is yours.

GROWING IN GENEROSITY

We've covered a lot of spiritual ground here so that you can see how your life has a unique purpose and place in our world. Because you are divinely created, and your fellow human beings are as well, we are all part of the family of our Creator, called to serve each other in love.

As part of honoring God and serving humanity, we have an obligation to also serve our physical environment and to be good stewards of the natural resources around us. This means respecting and caring for the land, water, air, and animals. Simply put, it's an attitude of love that demonstrates a deliberate care and appreciation for other people as well as the world we share.

Such an attitude of love can take many forms but often starts with simple acts of kindness and words of support. This may mean saying an encouraging word to someone new that you meet, making sure a loved one knows how much you care, giving a heartfelt hug to someone in pain, or providing resources for someone in need. It's a way of looking at each day as an opportunity to show God's love to everyone and everything you encounter. It may sound idealistic or out of touch with the harsh realities of our world, but I promise you it is not.

We are all in need in some way, and each of us has our struggles to deal with. Everyone with whom you come into contact is battling painful circumstances that they likely will not reveal to you. We all need each other. We all need kindness. We all need compassion and love.

There are many people and many needs, but start with at least one person. I have found that this is contagious, as the more you reach out to people in love and service, the more you will want to love others. Each person has an opportunity to serve through the giving of their time, talents, and treasure. Each of us has something to contribute in order to make a positive difference.

However, this is not an easy habit to develop. At times we either don't know how or what to give, we seem too busy to do so, or we don't want to be taken advantage of by others. Being generous is something that is learned, like any other worthwhile character trait. An attitude of generosity, of graciousness, of positive concern must be cultivated.

When humans are born, we are not by nature generous. Rather, we are self-consumed with survival, comfort, and someone meeting our needs. I don't know about you, but I have never seen a baby human who takes care of themselves and serves everyone around them in love, simply because they were born with a generous spirit. Rather, it takes time and instruction to learn about being generous, to truly serve others in love before yourself, and to care about making life better for another soul.

In my life, I decided to go on the long journey of learning to become more generous, more loving, and more empathetic with others. We all have burdens to bear, trials to go through, and pain to deal with. Life is not always easy, but it is always precious. You cannot truly understand what someone is going through unless it has happened the exact same way for you. This is rarely the case, though we are given trials and tribulations that can give us understanding, empathy, and compassion towards others if we truly learn a lesson through the process.

Consequently, instead of avoiding pain, I have learned to embrace it, to learn from it, to overcome it. This is not always easy or automatic, and many times it takes months or years to process it all. Once I am through the valley of darkness, I am able to have a better perspective, and usually I am presented with an opportunity to show love and understanding to someone who may be going through something similar. It often feels overwhelming, but when you focus on each day, each moment, each person, and each relationship, it's readily within reach. Our job is simply to listen, learn, love, and serve through that process.

FIRST FRUITS

For many years, I gave to various causes, ministries, charities, and individuals on a sporadic basis. Looking back, I probably regarded my giving like I would approach tipping for a meal. If things were going well and I could afford to give, then I did; if I was struggling and worried about the future too much, then I held back. But an attitude of loving generously requires a commitment to give consistently through all the ups and downs of life. This commitment relies on a foundation of eternal gratitude and not on temporary circumstances.

Giving is one of those things that can be a struggle for many of us. On one hand we don't want to be legalistic by setting our giving at a certain percentage of our income, and on the other hand we want to be faithful and honoring to the One who provides everything for us so generously. While the Bible gives us a good starting point at 10% of our resources (which was called a tithe in the Old Testament), ultimately I believe this a conversation to be had between you and God through honest prayer.

In the past, I noticed that my giving would occur after I paid all of my other bills. Since each of us can have a tendency to have our lifestyle match our income, or in some cases exceed our income and place us into debt, I never seemed to have enough to give away at the end of each month. When the offering plate would be passed at church on Sunday mornings, I would give from the money I happened to have in my pocket. Then later I became disappointed in myself to realize I spent more on the lunch afterwards with friends and family than on what went into that plate.

In wanting to be more faithful in my giving, I have embarked on an effort to truly give from "first fruits," another concept on giving established in the Old Testament of the Bible. In ancient times, when people would harvest their crops, they would give the first fruits of those crops as an offering to God as a way of honoring him first and showing their gratitude for the entire harvest he provided. Such an offering reinforced the concept that everything we have is God's and that he should be acknowledged and honored first for the amazing blessings he bestows upon us.

I realized the income I received was my "crop," and that unless I honored God by giving the "first fruits" to him, I was basically putting all my other wants and needs first and giving him leftovers, which is not how I want to give. Consequently, I decided to create a foundation that would receive the first percentage of my income, in an effort to be more accountable. Thus, the Brian Watson Foundation (www.brianwatsonfoundation.org) was born in 2014.

THE ART OF GIVING

Creating a foundation was not an easy decision for me, as Patricia and I have always conducted our giving from behind the scenes. This concept of giving without acknowledgment is biblical, but after much prayer and thought about the matter, I wanted to learn from other givers and to encourage others to join me in this journey of faithful stewardship and giving. Given that I have been fortunate in building a lot of relationships, I wanted to encourage people to give as a priority, a deliberate practice to illustrate our love for others and for our land and its resources. I wanted my foundation to ignite conversations with my friends and colleagues about giving so we could roll up our shirtsleeves together and make a positive difference in this world.

After much research, I elected to create a donor-advised fund through the National Christian Foundation. Without the time or massive resources to create my own autonomous foundation, I chose this route because I wanted my foundation's funds to serve those in need directly instead of being spent on overhead costs for operations. Many foundations can justify the expense of their operations, depending upon their level of contributions and goals, but for me, the donor-advised fund seemed like a good first step into the more structured world of giving.

The simplicity of this structure allows my fund to receive contributions from my investment deals. In addition, one hundred percent of the net sales proceeds payable to me from writing this book go directly to my foundation. The only profit I want from this book is knowing it has helped others—both readers willing to consider their own 7 Rings as well as others who benefit from the book's proceeds. I didn't write this book to make money, but rather to have a positive impact on the world.

I make recommendations to the fund administrators to give this money to organizations and people, which are in concert with my 7 Rings. Most of these donations go to people in need, faith-based initiatives, projects that support entrepreneurship, patriotic causes for American values, and education. By no means have I figured out the "art of giving," but I'm trying to do my best to keep taking steps on the journey.

In this journey, I love meeting other entrepreneurs who are either beginning to think about this concept of giving back or who seem to be masters at making a tremendous impact. I am a student of each, as I want to learn as much as I can to become a better steward, someone who is wise in how he gives, all so I can make the most positive sustainable impact possible in the lives of others.

This responsibility means being environmentally conscious, respecting life, making our air, water, and land clean and healthy, and leaving this world a little bit better than we found it. This does not mean that the environment has to be in conflict with humanity and its growth, as both can work in concert together. Without this planet and a sustainable environment, we cannot survive as a species. To respect human life, we must respect the environment.

Knowing your place in the world includes being a good steward of our environments and having a healthy love and respect for nature and all physical life around us. God gave us this planet, and we are responsible for caring for it and each other as an act of gratitude that glorifies him.

RING OF TRUTH
7 QUOTATIONS TO CONSIDER

"The earth will not continue to offer its harvest, except with faithful stewardship. We cannot say we love the land and then take steps to destroy it for use by future generations." | **Pope John Paul II**

"The master of the garden is the one who waters it, trims the branches, plants the seeds, and pulls the weeds. If you merely stroll through the garden, you are but an acolyte." | **Vera Nazarian**

"When a man becomes a Christian, he becomes industrious, trustworthy and prosperous. Now, if that man when he gets all he can and saves all he can, does not give all he can, I have more hope for Judas Iscariot than for that man!" | **John Wesley**

"The thing that lies at the foundation of positive change, the way I see it, is service to a fellow human being." | **Lee Iacocca**

"At the end of life we will not be judged by how many diplomas we have received, how much money we have made, how many great things we have done. We will be judged by 'I was hungry, and you gave me something to eat, I was naked and you clothed me. I was homeless, and you took me in.'" | **Mother Teresa**

"Everybody can be great...because anybody can serve. You don't have to have a college degree to serve. You don't have to make your subject and verb agree to serve. You only need a heart full of grace. A soul generated by love." | **Martin Luther King Jr.**

RING OF HONOR

QUESTIONS FOR REFLECTION

Do you believe that you are uniquely and divinely created?

_____

_____

_____

_____

_____

Has anyone ever told you that you are massively loved by the Creator of the entire Universe? If so, do you truly believe this? How does such a belief in God's love impact the way you live each day? What do you need to change in your daily habits in order to align your behavior with your beliefs?

_____

_____

_____

_____

_____

How can you serve others in love? How can you be the hands and feet of God to others around you? What's one need you can fill for someone this week?

_____

_____

_____

_____

_____

What does it look like to be a good steward of the environment? How can you help make the world a better place for future generations?

_____

_____

_____

_____

_____

If you could make one change to make the most positive impact in the world, what would this be? What is stopping you from doing this?

_____

_____

_____

_____

_____

CHAPTER 8

THE SEVENTH RING:
THE GIFT OF WORK

"Far and away the best prize that life offers is the chance to work hard at work worth doing." | **Theodore Roosevelt**

During the summers all through high school, I raised hogs and sheep for the Montrose County Fair. Next to my fishing worm business, which was the first "company" I ever created when I was about eight years old, raising animals was my first "larger scale operation." In addition to raising the lambs from ewes I owned, each spring I would buy "bum" lambs, baby lambs a mother ewe would not accept for some reason. The bum lambs usually needed to be bottle fed with milk in my arms until they could start eating hay and grass on their own. I would have to buy all their food, feed and water them, walk them, and groom them until it was time to show them at our annual county fair. I learned how to do much of this through my involvement in 4-H and Future Farmers of America (FFA).

This enterprise taught me valuable business lessons at a young age: about saving money to cover your operating costs, working hard to take care of your investments every day, taking calculated risks, developing multiple avenues for income (in this case hogs as well as lambs), and marketing. After working hard to develop the quality of each animal all summer, I would select my best lamb and hog to show at the fair. I meticulously groomed each animal for the important showmanship competitions, and depending on how they each placed, I would then receive the proceeds from the big auction sale, in which members of the business community bid on the animals.

ANIMAL FARM

These experiences with animals taught me more than just the value of hard work. They also showed me how business could help invest in a community because the area farmers and businesses could have found less expensive animals than the ones at auction. But these business owners and community leaders did this (and continue to do it today) because they wanted to help support kids who worked so hard in addition to building good will and increasing exposure for their companies.

After the fair was done, I would sell my remaining animals to my family and friends for meat. People who hear me talk about raising these animals always ask me how I could raise newborn lambs or cute little piglets by bottle feeding them in my lap, only to have them become lamb cutlets or bacon by the end of the year. But in addition to viewing them as investments, this process also helped me understand and appreciate the full circle of life. I gave these animals a good quality of life while they were with me, frequently reminding myself they were assets and not pets. I viewed it as the best of both—I cared for the animals but I also benefited from the excellent care I provided.

Such is the nature of work, our final and Seventh Ring. Many people look at my passion for Northstar and my excitement for new venture growth opportunities, and they assume I place work in one of my top rings. However, as you can see, it comes after the other six. This placement is deliberate for a number of reasons. By having business as the last and outer ring in my life, it helps to provide the financial resources to fuel and support the other six internal rings. It also helps me maintain focus on my true priorities and not merely on the temporal shifts of the economy or my net worth.

Early in life I heard the saying that you can learn a lot about someone's true priorities by looking at the entries in their checkbook and calendar. From my experience and observations, this holds true. People invest their time and money where they are most engaged. Consequently, the outer rings should help to support the inner, preceding rings, and in this case, the financial blessings from my business help to honor God and to provide for my wife, children, family, friends, community, the environment, and our great country.

With God at the center in the first ring, this kind of giving becomes natural, with the focus being to serve and love others. As we discussed in Chapter 7, giving from the first fruits keeps the focus on our gift as a gratitude rather than an obligation, thus removing any feelings of guilt or not being good enough. This perspective also changes one's mindset of only "giving from what is left" after paying other bills, or focusing on serving one's own needs instead of considering those of others.

SWEETER SUCCESS

As you'll recall from my story, I graduated from the University of Colorado with a Bachelor of Sciences degree with an emphasis in real estate. When my dream of joining the Peace Corps fell through, I was forced to come up with a Plan B, which was naturally related to real estate. Growing up in an entrepreneurial family involved in real estate investment and construction, I naturally gravitated to this field of business.

My parents had sold their campground, riding stables, and hunting preserve in upstate New York when I was young, and carried back the loan for the buyers. For many years my parents received a check in the mail each month from the new owners. Though it wasn't a big check, it was still a check that represented ongoing income for their hard work, personal sacrifices, and risk taking in owning and operating a business together for many years.

This arrangement resonated with me as a young man and inspired my approach to working. The value of thinking creatively, taking calculated risks, creating opportunities for others, and building residual income streams that would benefit me for many years regardless of my career status increased the older I got. Just the idea that I could have investments in properties that paid me while I was working elsewhere, on vacation, off fishing and hunting, or at my children's sporting events intrigued me.

This idea may have been born by seeing my parents always at work or not having as much time for us as children, especially during the busy summer months when the campsite was full. Given this background and experience, I always wanted to be an entrepreneur and build my own wealth within my own lifetime.

In my younger years, I might have wished I had been born into a wealthy family that would have given me greater financial support and security, but as I matured, I became glad I was not. I have greatly enjoyed the beautiful opportunity to work hard and to gain wisdom, to build wealth as the fruit of my own labors and not my ancestors'. In fact, I find this makes the journey sweeter, more enjoyable, and deeply rewarding. In addition, there is great security and confidence in knowing that if you built something once, you can build it again. If something is given to you for free, you may not appreciate its value unless you lose it and you may always be scared of losing it since you didn't create it. Because you did not pay anything for it, and did not sacrifice or give up something to attain it, you may not appreciate or value it as much. The same goes for money.

If you come from humble means and have the opportunity to work hard to attain your version of success, then you will be more fulfilled by your efforts. The harder you work, the sweeter your success. And keep in mind your success may come in different forms and differ from others' definitions. If you haven't already, be as specific and personal as possible about what success looks like and means to you, and then pursue it with passion. Through your hard work, blood, sweat, and tears, you can make something out of nothing.

Think about this for a minute. You have the ability to work hard and be rewarded for your contribution to this world. The harder and smarter you work, the more potential rewards you can secure for yourself and for others. You can help build a bridge, start a company, heal a sick person, or be the voice and hands of love in service to the world.

There are countless options before you, and you get the opportunity to choose. No one can take this away from you, unless you let them. You have the power to decide, to create, to build, or to tear down. There are builders as well as destroyers in this life—which will you be? This is an awesome opportunity and must never be taken for granted or squandered because of the expectations of others. The proverbial "tyranny of the urgent" will always try to pull you away from a long-term big picture so you must set your goals and chart your course.

FREEDOM TO DREAM

After being a commercial real estate broker from 1993-2000 at Cushman and Wakefield of Colorado, I had gained confidence from my experiences. Not only had I learned a good part of the business, but I had built relationships with some key people, and learned "the art of the deal" in an environment where I had to "hunt and kill" (since my salary was 100% commission-based) in order to eat. Those years taught me many valuable lessons about real estate values, the psychology of human beings, and how to lead in the midst of change and challenges.

Always striving to reach the next level, by 2000 I decided to take a step backward from the comfortable lifestyle we were building in order to take a giant leap forward in establishing my own company, Northstar Commercial Partners. Other than starting my childhood worm business and then later raising and selling animals, I had no real experience in launching a new company. Looking back, I find it encouraging to remember that I took on such a monumental endeavor as a newly married twenty-seven year old husband and father of two young children. Many probably asked, who was I to take on such a dream, such a responsibility, such a risk? And yet, why wait? I knew there would never be a perfect time so I decided to go for it.

Even though I knew the learning curve would be sharp, it turned out to be as sheer and steep as a Colorado black-diamond ski slope with lots of bumps. In those first days of starting a new business, I didn't know anything about the laws, regulations, personnel, or capital needed for our investment deals. Despite this crash-course education, I embraced my new adventure and just took it one step at a time.

Northstar has grown considerably over the past sixteen years. Now we own several million square feet of office, industrial, and retail properties and several land sites under separate investment entities in seventeen states across America. The company has been positioned as one of the key buyers of vacant and/or distressed properties that we reposition and improve, consequently creating jobs and stimulating growth in local communities.

Northstar Commercial Partners also allows me the opportunity to live out my faith and to serve in the real world, every day. The more Northstar grows and succeeds, the more I want to give back so that others may experience opportunities to pursue their dreams. Everyone should have a chance to pursue freedom, dignity, respect, opportunity, and empowerment for themselves. As President Ronald Reagan once said, "The American dream is not that every man must be level with every other man. The American dream is that every man must be free to become whatever God intends he should become." This is the business that Northstar is in, and real estate just happens to be the platform that we have been given to effect this positive change and impact.

POWER TO PERSEVERE

As I've shared with you, success has not come without great sacrifice and a commitment to persevere through life's challenges: experiencing the divorce of my parents, being uprooted from my home and family to move to Colorado when I was young, losing my stepfather when I was sixteen and having to become the man of the house very quickly, putting myself through college by shoveling horse stalls and working constantly, and starting my own company with no investors or help from my parents. However, if you recall how I started this book, then you know one of the hardest challenges in recent times was the Great Recession of 2008.

Prior to 2008, Northstar had never faced loan defaults, painful employee terminations due to the economy, or judgments by the courts. During this horrific time when the capital markets crashed, banks and financial institutions collapsed and many hard-working people lost their life savings and went into personal bankruptcy, we suffered as well. During this period, a few lenders wanted full payment of their real estate and business loans, as they too were receiving immense financial pressure from federal regulators, their boards of directors, and other constituents. All of this flowed down to us, as they demanded the payoff of loans, when the real estate values had plummeted and there were no buyers at reasonable prices.

As the manager of each investment company, it was my responsibility to do what was in the best interest of the equity investors, even if it was to my detriment personally. As a requirement of each loan, I had personally guaranteed the debt since our main business model was acquiring vacant real estate buildings that lenders perceived as higher risks. Consequently when the market crashed, our purchased properties would not lease or sell, which caused a few lenders to call some loans due.

In addition to the real estate issues, I had invested in two other Colorado-based companies, Peak Party Rentals and Aspen Moving and Storage. Both were also hit extremely hard by the economic collapse. Though we infused hundreds of thousands of dollars into these companies and other ventures, and never took a dime out, we could not keep them going, and eventually lost them and all of our invested capital. This was partly due to an unscrupulous manager of the companies, who elected not to pay employee payroll taxes and a host of other important bills, all without my knowledge. Since I did not actively manage or operate these companies and didn't even sign the checks, I was completely unaware of what he had done until it was too late.

Upon learning of the unethical behavior we terminated his employment, but too much damage had already been done. Even though I was not personally responsible for these debts as a member of a Limited Liability Company (LLC), I elected to pay $106,000 to the IRS to help address part of the employee payroll tax issue. Even though $106,000 is a lot of money at any time, this occurred at an extremely low point of the economy, when $106,000 felt like $106,000,000. We had very little money to pay our employees at other companies we owned, or for the real estate deals that required money to keep them afloat, so this was another extremely painful experience.

Though times were very tough, we worked hard with each lender to fight through this time together with them. We could not pay every lender all of the money they wanted at that moment, but we were committed to getting everyone paid over time. For those that worked with us, they eventually were paid, and a vast majority would do loans with us today.

However, for whatever reason some lenders couldn't or wouldn't work with us, and they sought court actions and judgments, which they secured on me personally as the guarantor after the investment entity could no longer cover its financial obligations. Consequently, I had to work out payment plans or settlements with these lenders, and I ended up paying millions of dollars personally to satisfy these judgments, as our investors were immune from this liability. Though many attorneys at that time told me to simply declare personal bankruptcy and walk away from those debts, I refused and worked tirelessly to satisfy these obligations and rebuild my company and its standing.

At this time, my wife and I lost *all* of our life's savings and net worth, which we had spent over ten years building together through hard work and personal sacrifice. Almost overnight, our net worth was millions of dollars *below* zero, given the obligations we had to meet of each investment entity, which exceeded what investors had put into those deals. So we placed every personal asset we owned up for sale, including our home and my childhood-dream car that I had found in a barn and restored: a 1961 Corvette convertible. None of our material possessions mattered, as we only hoped and prayed to sell what we could to meet the demands of these creditors, who remained relentless with their teams of attorneys, legal notices, and demands.

Sadly, we had to terminate people from the employ of Northstar, as we could not afford personally paying in excess of $100,000 per month to meet payroll and other business expenses, even though we had been doing this for many months after the Great Recession began. Many of my peers and mentors told me it was a big mistake to keep paying the salaries of these employees while my wife and I didn't get paid (that happens often as an entrepreneur and business owner, as you must put your employees first), but these people were like family, and I would rather sacrifice myself than them. Unfortunately, eventually we had no more money to pay them and had completely depleted our reserves, savings accounts, IRA, and equity in our home, while selling everything we could.

We were left with two employees, and vowed to find a way to work our way through it, or let God take it all away and have us go in any direction he wanted. During this time, my wife Patricia was a Godsend. With her legal background and amazing mind, she helped in phenomenal ways. We each worked fourteen-plus hour days, almost seven days a week, for several years to pull out of the morass. I truly could not have done this without her, and our marriage (Ring 2) grew even stronger because of it. We did not define our lives or relationship by these issues or financial circumstances, but rather committed to work hard to overcome them, if we could.

I share these details with you not for sympathy, but to remind you that in order to reach the mountaintops of success you usually have to pass through valleys of tribulation and darkness in this life. Regardless of the challenges you may encounter or are already facing, I encourage you to define and focus on what is truly important, and to embrace your challenges and fears rather than trying to avoid them. Past struggles have made me more empathetic to others, wiser, stronger, and a person who appreciates the blessings in life, both large and small.

SUCCESS TO SIGNIFICANCE

Though Northstar has grown much larger and stronger than where we were before the Great Recession, we remember our history and our roots, and continue to build wisely upon the foundation with which we have been entrusted. As we reached new heights, I became determined to channel our success into opportunities for the success of others. One of my greatest inspirations was a book I had read years ago, *Halftime* by Bob Buford.

The author shared his story of becoming a very successful businessman who had reached and exceeded his goals relatively early in life. As a result, he found himself no longer measuring his success by budgets and bottom lines but by the impact he and his companies were having to improve people's lives and to make an eternal positive difference. When he began pursuing this transformation from "success to significance," Buford discovered many other men and women with similar stories and similar desires to make a difference. He coined the term "halftime" to refer to the point where this shift occurs, regardless of one's age.

Knowing my stepfather Bill Watson passed away when he was only 42, I realized none of us know when our life's literal "halftime" will occur. Consequently, I should live my life to make the most of every day, not assuming I'm in halftime but playing as if time is running out in the fourth quarter. As President Lincoln once observed, "And in the end it is not the years in your life that count, it's the life in your years."

Though I am unsure how much time may be left on my personal clock, I should live life to the fullest, try to positively impact and bless others daily, and live my life with the goal to hear my Lord say on that day when we meet: "Well done, good and faithful servant." To me, this would be a life well lived, a life in which I know I've made the most of the abundant gifts and resources that have been entrusted to me.

With this goal of significance in mind, Northstar is in the community-building and people-empowering business, as we love to build meaningful and lasting relationships that provide dignity and benefit others. We know we can do well by doing good, and we always focus first on how we can create a positive impact for other people. In addition to the vacant buildings we purchase and redevelop, we have also acquired and repositioned environmentally impacted assets (Ring 5), assets for communities like AfrikMall (Ring 4), a center for the African immigrant community, and an Education Opportunity Fund (Ring 3), which buys vacant buildings for K-12 schools in America, especially in urban areas. Each of these focuses on a specific community or need, but all are tied together by creating opportunity, freedom, and empowerment for people.

I encourage you to consider your life from the same perspective. Make every day count toward a lasting legacy of positive change. No matter who you are, no matter what you do in this world, you have an amazing opportunity to bless someone in love this very day, and every day thereafter by giving of your time, talents, and treasure. This could mean saying a kind word, helping someone in need, listening to someone's story or troubles, or holding someone's hand in the park.

Each opportunity has been uniquely given to you. You are the one person put in your specific place, with your specific experiences, relationships, and position. If you don't act upon serving someone in love, who will?

If you are a follower of Jesus, you are the hands, feet, and body of Jesus. Go out and serve *all* people, especially those who may be different from you. Be known for your love and service towards others, no matter the cost, the loss, recognition, or the gain. In doing this one by one, we could transform the world for the better, and even if we don't transform an entire world, you will be blessed if you can benefit one life for the better. You may end up positively impacting hundreds or thousands of people, but always focus on helping to improve the one life first.

COURAGE TO CONTINUE

As mentioned, I am a big fan of great quotes. While in high school, soon after unexpectedly losing my stepfather, I found this quote, which is held in my business binder every day where I can see it: "Success is not final; failure is not fatal: It is the courage to continue that counts." Its author, Sir Winston Churchill, certainly knew something about facing adversity, overcoming obstacles, and persevering to victory.

His words remind me every day that I can improve. It also reminds me that the only true failure in life is to never try at all. In fact, I'm convinced some of our greatest successes come when we confront what the world may perceive as failures. Some people in this world will constantly judge, hate, and destroy, but it should be our response to love, to serve, and to build in spite of them. Through this process, we gain understanding, wisdom, and empathy for others.

If you truly try to learn the lesson from whatever you are going through, you may be given the opportunity to help someone else with a similar struggle they are having in the future. Don't sweep your perceived failures or problems under the carpet. Embrace them, learn from them. They will make you a better, stronger, and more authentic person than you would ever be without them.

Don't doubt yourself. When you pass from this life, you may think more about what you didn't do than what you did do. Live a life of adventure. Drink deep in the richness of love, family, friends, and nature. You only have one life to live in this world, make it truly count. To this end, I found this quote when I was a young man, which later was framed and became the first gift that my wife Patricia ever gave to me. It hangs on my office wall to this day, with a beautiful handwritten note of encouragement from her on the backside of the picture frame:

ITHACA

As you set out for Ithaca
hope your road is a long one,
full of adventure, full of discovery.
Laistrygonians, Cyclops,
angry Poseidon—don't be afraid of them:
you'll never find things like that on your way
as long as you keep your thoughts raised high,
as long as a rare excitement
stirs your spirit and your body.
Laistrygonians, Cyclops,
wild Poseidon—you won't encounter them
unless you bring them along inside your soul,
unless your soul sets them up in front of you.
Hope your road is a long one.
May there be many summer mornings when,
with what pleasure, what joy,
you enter harbors you're seeing for the first time;
may you stop at Phoenician trading stations
to buy fine things,
mother of pearl and coral, amber and ebony,
sensual perfume of every kind—
as many sensual perfumes as you can;
and may you visit many Egyptian cities

to learn and go on learning from their scholars.
Keep Ithaca always in your mind.
Arriving there is what you're destined for.
But don't hurry the journey at all.
Better if it lasts for years,
so you're old by the time you reach the island,
wealthy with all you've gained on the way,
not expecting Ithaca to make you rich.
Ithaca gave you the marvelous journey.
Without her you wouldn't have set out.
She has nothing left to give you now.
And if you find her poor, Ithaca won't have fooled you.
Wise as you will have become, so full of experience,
you'll have understood by then what these Ithacas mean.

C. P. CAVAFY (1863–1933)

RING OF TRUTH
7 QUOTATIONS TO CONSIDER

"Opportunities don't happen. You create them." | **Chris Grosser**

"Don't be afraid to give up the good to go for the great." | **John D. Rockefeller**

"There are two types of people who will tell you that you cannot make a difference in this world: those who are afraid to try and those who are afraid you will succeed." | **Ray Goforth**

"Successful people do what unsuccessful people are not willing to do. Don't wish it were easier; wish you were better." | **Jim Rohn**

"The ones who are crazy enough to think they can change the world, are the ones that do." | **Anonymous**

"People who succeed have momentum. The more they succeed, the more they want to succeed, and the more they find a way to succeed. Similarly, when someone is failing, the tendency is to get on a downward spiral that can even become a self-fulfilling prophecy." | **Tony Robbins**

"Don't let the fear of losing be greater than the excitement of winning." | **Robert Kiyosaki**

RING OF HONOR

QUESTIONS FOR REFLECTION

If you could create any company, business, or product, what would that be? What's keeping you from taking the first step?

_____

_____

_____

_____

_____

What is the most challenging or disappointing thing you have experienced in your career? What have you learned from it? Do others know about it, or is it a cage that you are locked into? Think about sharing this with someone, or writing it down. This may help to free you.

_____

_____

_____

_____

_____

During your most challenging times, who are your friends and mentors that can help guide you?

_____

_____

_____

_____

If you lost every material possession today, what would you do? Does this change who you are as a person?

_____

_____

_____

_____

_____

What is the one thing that is holding you back from pursuing the dream of your heart? What can you do to remove this roadblock, so you can impact the world for the better?

_____

_____

_____

_____

_____

CHAPTER 9

CONNECTING THE 7 RINGS:
THE GIFT OF LEADERSHIP

"If your actions inspire others to dream more, learn more, do more and become more, you are a leader." | **John Quincy Adams**

Throughout my life, I have naturally gravitated to positions of leadership. I don't know why this is a natural tendency for me, but I suppose it's simply the way I'm wired. It's not that I want to control anyone or be the one in charge; it's just that I want to contribute to positive change rather than waiting around for the impact of someone else's decisions. I want to be the best I can be and to empower others, and this drive for excellence seems to attract people who also strive to make their lives count as much as possible.

Though I held many leadership roles in high school, as President of the Honor Society, President of Future Farmers of America (FFA), Head Boy of Olathe High School (student body president), and many other roles in sports and various groups, I did not comprehend or study the differences in leadership styles until I was in college. Because I had to figure out how to put myself through college financially, given my mother's limited finances after my stepfather Bill Watson passed away, I filled out every scholarship application for which I was eligible.

Although I was very fortunate in getting many academic, community service, and leadership scholarships, one would change my life forever: being accepted to the President's Leadership Class (PLC) at the University of Colorado at Boulder. I still marvel at what a gift this special program played in my life at such a crucial time of development. Looking back, I see how this uniquely challenging program helped me in three distinct ways.

First, it made the immense CU campus more manageable and less intimidating for a small-town kid from the Western Slope of Colorado, mostly because there were only about sixty students accepted into this program (more than my graduating class of fifty-two back in Olathe). These students were all leaders of their high schools or held positions of leadership in other capacities, and PLC brought these like-minded overachievers together to study and develop the idea of leadership in our own lives.

Next, this class exposed me to the many different ideas and methods of leadership throughout history and across cultures around the world. All through high school I had practiced a leadership style of trying to do everything myself, not yet grasping the way true leadership always encourages and empowers others to do great things. Like anything worthwhile, leadership can be learned and developed in each person. Through understanding the various theories and methods of leadership,

I was able to identify and develop the methods that worked best for me. With a clearer understanding of my natural strengths, I could then empower others to exercise their own natural strengths as well.

Finally, PLC taught me to seek out all different types of people to learn from, to emulate, to collaborate with—and then to grow with them. This kind of leadership embraces diversity and isn't afraid to confront and integrate a variety of views. This integrative style of leadership is not always easy to practice because it's usually easier, or feels more natural, to gravitate toward others who are similar to us. It's not difficult to lead other people if they already agree with us and automatically defer to our decisions.

However, a homogenous style of leadership quickly becomes stale and even dangerous because those around us only reinforce our same beliefs and methods. Consequently, we lose a precious treasure—the ability to see issues, problems, opportunities, and solutions through multiple perspectives. This type of leader isn't threatened by those who disagree with them; instead they welcome the stimulation that comes from diverse cultural collaboration. This was the kind of leader I wanted to become.

LEADERSHIP LEARNING CURVES

I'm often asked if there's a secret to my leadership style, or if there's one particular leader I seek to emulate more than any other. While I have many different role models for my style of leadership, I believe each of us is gifted to lead in a way that's uniquely our own. If there's any secret to the way I lead, it's simply a willingness to engage with each day, each person, each opportunity before me. I value being a servant leader. I try to surrender my expectations while also being as fully informed as possible.

Balancing this kind of leadership attitude is not always easy. But this is where the 7 Rings provides such a powerful scaffold for a person's ability to lead. When your life is balanced in all major areas, you're free to serve others through your leadership.

After graduating from CU, I entered the full-time work force as I shared with you earlier. Choosing to work in commercial real estate for such a large firm as Cushman and Wakefield, and then later launching my own company as Northstar Commercial Partners, I often experienced sharp learning curves. In other words, I made a lot of mistakes and experienced the normal ups and downs we all encounter in our careers. But I worked hard to learn from each and every one of them, especially the most challenging ones.

In addition to learning from my mistakes and missteps along the way, I have tried to embrace every leadership opportunity that has come my way. Obviously, there are limits to our time and energy, but I intuitively understood the best way to hone and to maximize my leadership skills was to lead and encourage others in a variety of contexts and situations. Through the years I have continued to embrace many various leadership roles, and today my bio includes:

- Founder and CEO of Northstar Commercial Partners and Northstar Commercial Management;
- Founder and CEO of The Brian Watson Foundation;
- Co-founder and Principal of Xcel Companies, an expense-reduction company for corporate payment processing, print/promotional materials, and shipping/mail costs;
- President and member of the Leadership Program of the Rockies 2015 Class;
- Chairman of the LPR Retreat Finance Committee and member of the Board of Directors;
- Board member of the Colorado Commission on Family Medicine

for the 6th Congressional District of Colorado appointed by the Governor of Colorado;

- Leadership Council Member for the Colorado National Federation of Independent Business (NFIB);
- Member of The Colorado Association of Commerce and Industry (CACI), also known as the Colorado State Chamber of Commerce;
- Member of the Chairman's Roundtable while serving on the Energy and Environment Council and the Governmental Affairs Council;
- A-List Member of CXO, a private collaborative executive organization of influence that connects C-level executives and owners of companies throughout the world;
- Founder and CEO of the Opportunity Coalition, which promotes collaboration among the people of Colorado and new business startups to create quality jobs throughout our state; Former board member and active supporter of the Tragedy Assistance Program for Survivors (TAPS) for those who have lost loved ones in U.S. Military Service;
- Chairman of the Finance Committee for the Colorado Republican Party;
- Member of the Board of Governors and President's Council for Opportunity International, one of the world's largest microfinance lenders providing loans to individual entrepreneurs in the developing world;
- Executive Committee Member of the International Board of Directors for Mercy Ships, the world's largest non-profit medical hospital on a traveling ship, which performs over 60,000 annual life changing surgeries for free in Africa;
- Republican delegate for my County, Congressional, and State political assemblies;
- Board Member and President of Brokers Benefiting Kids, a Denver based non-profit that raises financial support for multiple children's charities in Colorado;

- Member of the Metro Denver Executive Club;
- Member of the Legacy Political Organization;
- Member of the Citywide Banks Advisory Board;
- Member of the Republican Business Advisory Council;
- Chairman of the Advisory Board for the Alliance for Choice in Education, a Denver-based non-profit that provides educational scholarships and school choice programs for low-income students grades K-12;
- Chairman of The Board of Directors and a mentor for Save Our Youth, a Denver-based inner city youth mentoring program;
- President and member of the Downtowner's Toastmasters Club;
- President of Homeowner's Association for Capitol Hill Neighborhood in Denver;
- Board member for the Colorado Coalition for the Homeless;
- Board member of the Aurora Economic Development Council;
- Founder and host of *The Mountains of Opportunity,* a TV show that airs positive stories of entrepreneurs and job creators of all types of small and large businesses throughout Colorado.

I share this list of my various leadership positions with you not to brag or blow my own horn. I simply want to indicate both the variety of opportunities and organizations in which I've been privileged to serve and in some cases to lead, as well as to illustrate the common denominator for them all: servant leadership. You see, I'm convinced the only effective leadership serves the needs of others first and not the leader's ego.

SERVANT LEADERSHIP IN ACTION

While I've learned there are many different forms of this elusive quality called leadership, I remain firmly convinced the best, most effective, most far-reaching form is servant-based leadership. What does this mean? And better yet, what does this kind of leadership look like in action?

A servant-minded leader is one who cares, loves, sacrifices themselves, and genuinely wants to serve others. This type of leader cares more about the people or cause that they serve than about getting the credit, gaining absolute control, or "getting something in return." This is the type of person who puts others before themselves, who would willingly "take a bullet" for the team, who would try to save others before themselves. In the end, this person dares greatly, loves deeply, and empowers people to achieve their dreams of success. In the end, this leader realizes that this life is temporary, and that they have a duty to carry on possibility and potential to the next generation.

I aspire to be a great servant leader. I have much to learn, but I try to exercise what this leadership style looks like, in as many interactions and roles as I can. My role model for such revolutionary others-first leadership remains the greatest servant leader of all-time: Jesus. If you think about it, this is a man who was born in a manger, didn't come from a wealthy or powerful family, came instead from Galilee (an area many looked down upon as provincial or even backward), worked as a carpenter, and acquired no wealth or military power. And yet Jesus continues to transform the world thousands of years after his death at the age of thirty-three. How in the world did he do this?

I'm convinced Jesus was the greatest servant leader because he led an authentic life, one that radiated consistent truth, compassion for *all* people, and immense love. There is never a time when Jesus went back on his word, lied, or deceived people in order to gain something. He was a man who often did and said things that did not make sense from a surface perspective but continue to resonate with timeless wisdom today.

Jesus was often radical yet dynamic, different and still mesmerizing. True, he had certain divine powers of healing and control over nature, but he also lived a difficult human existence, one that ended in suffering and death in ways that most of us cannot imagine and could never endure. Jesus started with twelve disciples, a mostly uneducated, un-travelled, un-tested lot, who would end up helping to spread a message of Good News that still transforms the world today.

Jesus was so impactful because he focused his efforts on being consistent, speaking truth even if it didn't appeal to everyone, and exercising constant love, empathy, and service to those around him. The latter is probably the most effective aspect of his ministry because I'm convinced the force of true love is more powerful than any other weapon devised against humanity. Love can and will conquer all, even when it does not appear to have the power to do so at times.

MORE FOR, LESS AGAINST

Today, Christianity is under attack. This is not a new phenomenon, as the faith has always been under attack, even during the ministry of Jesus, especially when he was beaten and crucified on a Roman cross. Jesus told his followers that they would encounter this kind of opposition and even persecution. This is partly our lot in life because our message of hope, love, and healing is counter to the forces of this world.

As a result, we will always receive ridicule and persecution, as the power structures of this world are directly threatened by a belief system that ascribes all glory, allegiance, and power to a higher being. No matter what force or negative barrier is imposed upon us, we will still love and serve God.

In addition, no person is withheld access to a relationship with Jesus, and for those who pursue control through coercion, this is threatening. As the Apostle Paul wrote in his letter to the Christians living in Rome, "If we live, we live for the Lord; and if we die, we die for the Lord. So, whether we live or die, we belong to the Lord" (Romans 14:8). As another reminder of this truth, I keep a framed version of Philippians 4:11 in my office, which states: "I have learned to be content whatever the circumstances."

If our model of a balanced life and of servant leadership is Jesus, then we can expect our life to be challenging at times. He made it very clear that we are to be first known for our love to our God, and second our love for our fellow human beings. Sadly, sometimes Christians are known more for what they are against than what they are for.

If you asked a random person on the street, "What do you think about Christians?" or "What are the top three things that come to mind when you hear the word Christian?", many people would tell you that they are "against abortion," "against homosexuality," "against people of other faiths or those who have no faith at all," on and on. How transformative would it be if those same people answered with: "Wow! Those Christians are the most loving and caring people I know!" or "Being a Christian is about truly loving and serving humanity, no matter the cost and with no worldly gain or recognition." Can you imagine?

I strive to be this kind of servant leader, one known for the way he brings service, healing, reconciliation, opportunities for growth, and freedom from oppression to those around him. You see, Jesus led a life of servant leadership, and he was known far and wide for his love, for his healing, for his service. This is the kind of leadership we must emulate, and this kind of leadership is the natural result of living according to the 7 Rings.

Unfortunately, I fear we often lose our focus and become distracted by the lure of power, wealth, status, and personal achievement. But this is not what life, or leadership, is all about. If Jesus came back today, would he recognize the people that call themselves his followers? Would he immediately seek out a big, brand new mega-church in the suburbs, or would he quickly go to an area that most self-respecting

Christians wouldn't dare approach on a Sunday, or for that matter, most any other day?

Clearly, we know the answer even if we don't always practice it. Jesus would be looking for the hurting, the lost, the oppressed, the disenfranchised, and lonely among us. He would be healing, listening, serving, and showing love and compassion to people you may not even like, trust, or know. He would be seeking out those who are the outcasts, the outsiders, the unwanted, and he would embrace each with love.

What if we did the same? What if each follower of Jesus committed to finding a handful of people in their lives with whom they could build authentic relationships of love and service without judgment? What a different world this would be!

This kind of servant leadership would help to transform the world in an amazingly powerful and positive way. We would truly be living out the Lord's commandment to love our God with all of our heart, mind, and soul, and to serve our neighbors as ourselves. This is true servant-based leadership, and it starts in your home, with your family, and grows in your communities. This is not about conversion or coercion, but about simple acts and words of love and kindness to our fellow human beings.

COMMON THREADS

Servant leadership is the natural result of living according to the 7 Rings. When you put all 7 Rings together, the combined strength of them working in synchronicity together will change your life in many positive ways. While no one is perfect, and no one's life is without tragedy and unexpected losses, using the 7 Rings can provide balance and perspective and unleash more joy, peace, and fulfillment in your life. When you experience the harmony of having your life in balance, then you can experience a contentment few people rarely achieve.

When your life is balanced and your priorities are clear, then life's decisions aren't nearly so challenging. This kind of balance liberates you to lead in a way that welcomes change and invites dialogue with a diversity of opinions. This is the secret to life-changing, people-empowering, community-building servant leadership.

Woven throughout the 7 Rings are many "common threads," truths that illustrate ways of working, serving, and leading other people. These are lessons I've learned over the years, and here are fifty of my favorites that I hope will ignite your own servant leadership. These are the gifts of leadership, the fruit of a life lived by the 7 Rings.

1. Be authentic and real in interactions with others.
2. Build quality relationships with people.
3. Spend time with those you care about, and time with those that may be different from you, as you can learn a lot from both.
4. Make sure that you live each day as if it could be your last, as it just may be.
5. Never be afraid to show or receive love, even with people who have hurt you.
6. Honor your parents, and call them often to tell them that you love them.
7. Do the same with your siblings, even if you don't always get along.
8. Make your word your bond, even when it is hard or easy not to.
9. A reputation for honesty, integrity, and fair dealing is hard won, and easily lost.
10. One of the true measures of a person is how they treat people that they have nothing to gain anything from.
11. Be respectful.

12. Honor holy places, even if they may not be holy to you.

13. Take time to spend in quiet places.

14. Think. Think. Think.

15. Ask questions, even tough and uncomfortable ones, as they will help you grow.

16. Read as much as you can, from all types of different sources. Knowledge is a form of power, and the more you learn the stronger you will be.

17. Exercise. Often.

18. Be sure to eat more salads and less sandwiches for lunch.

19. Find out what you love doing, and make it your profession. If you love what you do for a living, you will never have to work another day in your life.

20. Focus on serving others in authentic, meaningful, and positively transforming ways.

21. Ask people of all types to tell you their story, especially taxi cab drivers in New York City. You will learn a lot, and be richly blessed by conversations with them.

22. Hold the door open for people.

23. Say please and thank you, as much as you can.

24. Each day that you awake, you can decide to be happy, sad, or mean. Focus on being happy, as people will like you a lot more. This happiness with others will lead to joy.

25. There is always someone who is dealing with something more challenging than you. Keep perspective, as there are many who don't even have that capability any longer.

26. Explore the answer to this question every day: How do I know God exists?

27. Be patriotic to your country and thank veterans and current military personnel for their service each time you see them.

28. It is ok to cry, and to laugh. Don't be afraid or unwilling to show your emotions.

29. Love your pets, especially if you have a dog.

30. Spend quality time with your spouse and kids. These are priceless gifts that may not always be with you.

31. Travel to other cities, states, and countries. There is a big world out there, and there are so many great people to meet, exotic foods to taste, and lands to see.

32. Be faithful. Be joyful. Be spontaneous.

33. Live life with an attitude of gratitude.

34. Be the friend that you wish you had.

35. Say yes more, and challenge yourself with new ideas.

36. Climb a mountain, swim in the ocean, or run through a meadow. Don't always be constrained.

37. Make your work challenging, and always strive for improvement.

38. Be informed about politics, and vote for the person that will make the most positive change.

39. Learn to cook, especially with your spouse.

40. Find someone to help or be kind to, every day.

41. At times, be still and content.

42. Take a moment to really appreciate the awe and beauty of this planet. To our knowledge, there is only one like it.

43. When you are at your lowest most challenging times, pray. Start this prayer with all the things you are thankful for, starting with the ability to touch, see, hear, taste, smell and work your way through

all the blessings you have been given. By the time you reach your challenging issue, you may have more perspective.

44. Always remember that you only have one life to live. Make it count.

45. Ask yourself what you would like to be remembered for, and live a life that is worthy of your true calling.

46. Money comes and goes, but relationships, rich experiences, knowledge, and love remain if you cultivate them. Place your focus on those things that will last.

47. Try to figure out how you can make the world a better place than when you found it, and work to make that happen.

48. Give at least the first 10% of your income to God and to those in need, save and invest the next 10%, and live on the remaining 80%, if possible.

49. Hold people accountable, but be willing to forgive and forget.

50. Never give up hope. Never.

RING OF TRUTH
7 QUOTATIONS TO CONSIDER

"Service which is rendered without joy helps neither the servant nor the served. But all other pleasures and possessions pale into nothingness before service which is rendered in a spirit of joy." | **Mahatma Gandhi**

"Where there is no vision, the people perish." | **Proverbs 29:18**

"Before you are a leader, success is all about growing yourself. When you become a leader, success is all about growing others." | **Jack Welch**

"Never doubt that a small group of thoughtful, concerned citizens can change world. Indeed it is the only thing that ever has." | **Margaret Mead**

"The most dangerous leadership myth is that leaders are born-that there is a genetic factor to leadership. That's nonsense; in fact, the opposite is true. Leaders are made rather than born." | **Warren Bennis**

"Become the kind of leader that people would follow voluntarily; even if you had no title or position." | **Brian Tracy**

"Men make history and not the other way around. In periods where there is no leadership, society stands still. Progress occurs when courageous, skillful leaders seize the opportunity to change things for the better." | **Harry S. Truman**

RING OF HONOR

QUESTIONS FOR REFLECTION

What does servant based leadership mean to you? How would you apply this to your life to be the most effective?

_____

_____

_____

_____

_____

Who are some current leaders that have shown what it means to be a servant-based leader? Who are ones that have shown the opposite?

_____

_____

_____

_____

What do you admire most about the leadership qualities of Jesus? How does his example inspire you to lead differently than you're currently leading? Why?

_____

_____

_____

_____

If you could emulate one leader in the world, whether current or historical, who would be that be? What is it you admire most about them? Why?

_____

_____

_____

_____

_____

Review the list of "Common Threads" and circle the ones that speak to you most directly right now in your life. Which ones are your favorites? Why?

_____

_____

_____

_____

Please refer to page 204 of this book to write down your top 50 sayings or quotes—your own "Common Threads." Do you notice a current theme, or idea that resonates with you? What action do you need to take in order to exercise this truth in your life at present?

_____

_____

_____

_____

_____

CHAPTER 10

CHAMPIONSHIP RINGS:
HEROES, MENTORS, AND LEADERS

"It doesn't take a hero to order men into battle. It takes a hero to be one of those men who goes into battle." | **Norman Schwarzkopf**

People sometimes ask me what keeps my 7 Rings in a "balanced rotation" or "synchronous orbit" in my life. From my experience, the answer is relationships—and having heroes and mentors in my life. I continually draw strength, inspiration, encouragement, and support from the lives of men and women who have persevered and overcome adversity.

Some I may know only from the pages of history or the words they themselves penned; others I'm privileged to know personally. Many of my heroes are iconic leaders who inspire countless others by their courageous deeds and decisions. Others are "average people" quietly living their lives with integrity, kindness, and dignity. I'm convinced regardless of how you encounter them, you must have heroes and mentors in your life if you want to maximize the 7 Rings and enjoy a life of fulfilled purpose and servant leadership.

HOLDING OUT FOR A HERO

Lately superheroes seem to have overtaken the movie screens in most of our theaters. Whether they're battling each other, a global menace from another world, or an evil leader intent on destruction, superheroes have tapped into our innate human hunger for powerful role models, individuals who can show us how to triumph over adversity.

However, finding real heroes in our society has become increasingly difficult. Aided by the internet and social media, public individuals are scrutinized for their private weaknesses. Consequently, we have learned that our heroes have very human flaws; their strengths are often offset by their weaknesses. We are often left disappointed in the hero we once held so high.

This was my experience when I read the book *The Dark Side of Camelot* by Seymour Hersh. You see, John F. Kennedy had been a hero of mine since I was a young boy, but I learned that he was an extremely unfaithful husband to his wife. This made me want to give him up as a hero altogether after reading the book, but I came to realize that while his extensive infidelities disappointed me, he still contained other qualities of leadership worth admiring. Despite his moral failures, President Kennedy cast a vision that empowered the American people and energized our determination.

He is but one example of the way our leaders, like all human beings, are incredibly complex. We *all* have our shortcomings as well as our stellar achievements. Unfortunately, sometimes people try to "dig up the dirt" in order to discredit some amazing historical figures, including our

Founding Fathers as described earlier in this book.

These critics believe that if you can cast doubt on one aspect of a person's life, then you can discredit and throw out the entire person's contributions and beliefs. Such negative thinkers really want to deny the person's end results, and use whatever means they can to destroy them. This is also frequently used in politics today, as people try to focus on destroying the individual rather than having a civil discussion about the ideas and topics that really affect our country. As mentioned earlier, I have already experienced this personally when the opposition attacked me during the 2012 election.

Over the course of my life, I've learned it is often hard to find a "complete hero," one whom you would like to emulate in every part of your life. Rather, we can admire certain attributes from each hero or mentor, while also recognizing they struggled with certain weaknesses as we all do. We can respect the courage it took for them to make hard decisions and overcome adversity without allowing their mistakes to eclipse such achievements. We can be inspired by their bravery, fortitude, and perseverance in specific and limited ways without qualification and complete acceptance of all their actions.

EVERYDAY HEROES

Real heroes don't have to have X-ray vision, an iron suit, or the Batmobile in order to inspire us. Real heroes are simply people who use their gifts to live with purpose and integrity. They are the people we look up to, derive encouragement from, and emulate to create the life we would like to live. In my own journey, I have learned virtually anyone you meet can be a hero, capable of providing both insight and inspiration.

In fact, everyone you meet can teach you two important lessons: how they have arrived at their present position, role, or season of life; and also the source of hope, inspiration, and encouragement that has sustained them to this point. Many times people help us by sharing the stories of their mistakes, which may give us insight or wisdom so we can avoid the same ones in our own lives. Other times, they reveal their personal motivational fuel that keeps them going when it would be easier to give up.

Each person has a unique, special story, one revealing many lessons for us to learn. Whether they are a CEO, janitor, teacher, security guard, factory worker, mother, or child, everyday heroes have so much to teach us if we invest the time to take an interest in their lives. Lessons of simplicity, hard work, service, strength of will, and love can resonate in our own souls, helping us to become more understanding, empathetic, and compassionate.

Because of these lessons, I like keeping a list of heroes, mentors, and inspirational figures as fuel for my spirit. From time to time, I will review, edit, and add new individuals, but keeping the list reminds me to focus on being the best person I can be. I encourage you to do the same and consider who you would place in your personal "Heroes' Hall of Fame." Some may be famous or historical figures while others may only be known to you or a few people in your community.

HEROES' HALL OF FAME

To get you started, allow me to share some of the most important heroes and mentors I have in my life, with a brief explanation of what I have learned and continue to learn from each of them. Though it was difficult to select which ones to include here, I selected each to reflect a certain unique attribute or lesson that I have gleaned from them. Again, each person is unique, and though they may have made a positive impact in one area, they may not be the type of person I would want to be in other areas. Despite their limitations or flaws, each one can ignite the hero within us.

1) **_Jesus_**. Though there are many lessons one can learn from Jesus, some of the greatest include love, humility, peace, self-sacrifice, and servant-based leadership. Even without worldly attributes of money title, and power, the Son of God chose to humble himself and serve **all** of humanity through peaceful and radical love. In the end, Jesus gave the ultimate sacrifice for those he loved, his very life. This final act of death on a cross was his most powerful act of service to humanity. The very tool of his torture and death, the cross, became the symbol of salvation for his followers for centuries to come. What was meant for death became a symbol of life. What was meant to destroy and silence has instead helped to rebuild individual lives and humanity, while allowing the human soul to be restored and to feel its true worth.

2) **_Job_**. Found in the Old Testament of the Bible, Job's story may be familiar to you as one of long-suffering. Job was very prosperous and well respected, until Satan challenged God to take everything away from Job and test the man's faithfulness. So God allowed Satan to take everything away from Job—his possessions, wealth, family, friends, and health. After losing everything, Job remained faithful to God. He believed that since we praise God in the good times, we should also do so in the bad times: "Naked I came from my mother's womb, and naked I will depart. The Lord gave and the Lord has taken away; may the name of the Lord be praised" (Job 1:21). Due to his unfailing faith, the Lord ended up delivering Job from this state, and made him even more wealthy and prosperous than ever before. Whether the Lord gives us many possessions or we have nothing, it does not change the fact that God is Lord of the Universe, and it is our job to humbly accept, love, and serve him and others.

3) **_Solomon_**. In the Book of Ecclesiastes, which is my favorite book in the Bible after Job, King Solomon, the wealthiest king to ever live, provides perspective on what is truly meaningful in this life. After experiencing all the world has to offer, Solomon concludes that the key to true satisfaction is not immense wealth or self-gratifying experiences, but rather a true and meaningful relationship with the Lord. When a young man, God told Solomon he would grant him one request. Of all the things that Solomon could have asked for, he asked for wisdom. Solomon knew wisdom helps to identify and prioritize the goals that are truly meaningful and worthy in this life. True wisdom and discernment is a lifelong goal to which I aspire in my own life. Throughout all the ups and downs of his tumultuous life, Solomon understood that a relationship with the Lord was foundational.

4) **_George Washington_**. Many of us think of George Washington as the person who helped lead a ragtag army of revolutionaries against an immense British army. Though his fortitude, strength, and cunning in battle were undoubtedly impressive, it is his character traits after the war that I admire even more. For it was after the upstart Colonies defeated the mighty British that General George Washington had the opportunity to become a dictator, supreme commander, or monarch over the new American colonies. However, he chose to become our country's first president, and yield to the model of a constitutional republic. This choice took great self-constraint, and a belief in this new system of government by the people, which was largely untested. Washington's leadership on the battlefield, and in office as the First President of these new United States of America provided guideposts for each president that has come since, setting the bar for great service

to one's country. I wish we had more leaders that truly cared for and served the people rather than believing the people should serve them and their political careers or personal advancement.

5) ***Ernest Shackleton***. If you have not read the book *Endurance: Shackleton's Incredible Voyage* by Alfred Lansing, I recommend it highly. After setting records in sailing in the race to the South Pole during the Heroic Age of Antarctic Exploration, Shackleton focused on crossing Antarctica. His ship, *The Endurance*, became stuck in polar ice in 1914, and was torn apart. He and his crew had to camp on the polar ice, and then had to travel 720 miles to the South Georgia island. Through his leadership, each of his men was saved, enduring months of starvation and bitter cold. This is true sacrificial leadership, in spite of the harsh conditions. Today, Shackleton's name is synonymous with sacrificial leadership under the most adverse of circumstances. He is known more for how he handled a failed sailing expedition rather than what records he broke. He reminds me that sometimes the unexpected crisis or destructive moment may yield our greatest moments of accomplishment. We must remain open and perceptive even when our "ship" becomes grounded and torn apart by the iciness of this world. It may be our golden opportunity to leave the past behind, and to begin a treacherous but monumental journey of survival and true servant-based leadership.

6) **Abraham Lincoln**. A humble man of persistence and extraordinary leadership, Abraham Lincoln consistently defied the odds against him. Though he ran for office many times, it wasn't until the eighth time that he was elected President of the United States. Lincoln led our country at a time when it was being torn apart by civil war and a social divide over slavery. During extreme adversity, Lincoln demonstrated fortitude, consistency, and strength.

He understood the greater good of keeping the country unified, while acknowledging the rights that all people were created equal, had to be supported and protected. Even during the darkest periods of the war, Lincoln stayed the course. This commitment to what was right and just helped to transform our nation, and I believe eventually the world, for the better. This leadership style is not about taking polls, or swaying with the popular sentiment of the day, but taking necessary risks and having the fortitude to do what is right.

7) **_William Wilberforce_**. William Wilberforce served in the English Parliament from 1801-1812 and was the main voice and leader in the movement to abolish slavery. After living a life of gambling and debauchery, in 1785 Wilberforce experienced a life-changing conversion to Christianity. This conversion not only changed his personal life, but placed him on a lifelong journey to abolish slavery, which he deemed as unmoral and ungodly. Wilberforce helped to lead the Parliamentary campaign against the British slave trade for 26 years, until the The Slave Trade Act of 1807 was finally approved, and the final Slavery Abolition Act of 1833 was passed, which abolished slavery in most of the British Empire. I admire this man's personal transformation, and his focus on fighting and eliminating a widely accepted social convention due to his faith and moral convictions. Wilberforce's conversion is perhaps best described by "Amazing Grace," the hymn written by John Newton (1725-1807), the former captain of a slave trade ship. While enduring a violent storm at sea, Captain Newton wrote these famous lyrics, and subsequently gave his life to God:

Amazing Grace, how sweet the sound,
That saved a wretch like me.
I once was lost but now am found,
Was blind, but now I see.

This is one of those songs that brings tears to my eyes each time I sing it during a church service as it reminds me that even a wretch like me has hope, forgiveness, and salvation. It is a song I hope will be sung by my loved ones at my funeral service one day.

8) *John F. Kennedy*. JFK was the first "television president." He embodied a sense of pride and confidence in the American spirit. He challenged the American people to travel to the moon, and we did. I believe we need more great servant-based leaders who challenge us to reach for our metaphorical moons, to stretch beyond our own limitations and work together for the greater good. JFK's youth, charisma, and oration helped to challenge and encourage a country to reach beyond themselves in this service to others. His famous exhortation to "ask not what your country can do for you, but what you can do for your country" helped to strike a new chord in the American psyche about true service and commitment to the very ideals that make our nation so great. His words inspire me to this day, and I hope to inspire others in some small way through my actions and encouraging words.

9) *Mother Theresa*. Her heart for serving the poorest of the poor in India remains legendary. This woman—without wealth, title, or celebrity—accomplished more than most individuals can even imagine. She served with humility, grace, and compassion, always putting the needs of others before herself in true

unconditional love. She reminds me: "Spread love everywhere you go. Let no one ever come to you without leaving happier."

10) **_Rosa Parks_**. This woman dared to sit at the front of a bus in Birmingham, Alabama, at a time when such an act was socially unacceptable. Her courage and strength galvanized the need for social change and bolstered the Civil Rights Movement. I admire that Rosa Parks never set out to live a life of leadership or to become the lightning rod that would help to transform a nation. She simply took her seat at the front of a bus because she was tired and knew she had certain inalienable natural rights given to all of us, whether black or white, by our Creator. Her bold act helped to empower many others to speak out and to create the necessary change that would allow people to sit anywhere on the "bus of life" for decades to come. This is true courage. This is heroic strength. This is transformational change that helps to make the world a better place.

11) **_Ronald Reagan_**. There is so much to say about President Reagan, including the unwavering faith he held in the American people. He knew without a doubt our great nation is a place unlike any other. His charming, homespun quips helped to communicate his profound messages of timeless wisdom. When Reagan came into office, the failed policies of big government going astray had taken their toll. Unemployment was high and spirits were low, but these extremes did not sway this former actor from taking on the most important role of his life. Reagan was the right man, for the right moment, and we are better off today for him answering that call. In addition to his work on domestic issues, I admire Reagan for his strength of will in dealing with Communist Russia.

Through his willingness to "trust, but verify" and his persistent belief that freedom and capitalism trump communism, he finally broke down walls, both figurative and literal. His leadership created positive transformation in lives and helped to prove that certain economic and political systems work better than others.

12) ***Martin Luther King, Jr.*** As a follower of Jesus, a pastor, and a gifted orator, Dr. King communicated his messages with clarity and passion. And as a Republican, he helped to bring freedom to all people in our great land. His life was marked with challenges and change, but he had passion and purpose that led him to be a voice for others. Though King could have called for violent protests, his faith inspired him to protest through peaceful and rational means. It takes great strength, self-control, and faith to follow such a radical path, but this is what he did. Even while his life was in danger, King kept speaking the truth and empowering others with his words and actions. In the end, he lost his life for this cause, but he lives on in the memories of the masses, and in the better life that all of us have enjoyed due to his personal mission and sacrifice.

13) ***Billy Graham***. The Reverend Billy Graham is one of those humble souls who has always spoken truth with conviction. While "more famous" pastors got caught in sexual and financial scandals, Graham led a life of humility and service. This preacher introduced many people to Jesus, as he exemplified servant leadership. At the peak of his popularity, this man was probably the most famous person of faith in America. Such notoriety could have easily gotten to his head, as it has done with many people like him. However, Graham remained always faithful to God, focusing on sharing a message of Good News and hope to anyone

who would listen. Aware of his humble heart, the Lord blessed Graham with decades of effective ministry and an enduring legacy. I admire Graham's faith and purpose, as he is that tree mentioned in Psalm 1, growing deep and strong alongside the stream of life.

14) **_Thomas Jefferson_**. Jefferson was a well-read and knowledgeable Renaissance man. His ability to draft the Declaration of Independence and the Constitution of the United States of America reamins truly awe-inspiring. Jefferson truly embodies the "power of the pen" in how it can be used to help liberate people.

15) **_William Shakespeare_**. As stated earlier in this book, I've always been a big fan of Shakespeare's works. The intricacy and play on words, in the context of speaking out against the political, social, and economic powers of the time are amazing. Many writers have built upon the foundation of Shakespeare, and yet none have been able to replicate his utter genius and wit with the English language. Whether you believe that Shakespeare was a simple man born in Stratford-upon-Avon, or an insider of the Royal Court, his brilliance distilled the essence of the human condition—love, hate, fear, greed, jealousy, rage, grief, ambition, and forgiveness. No other writer has created so many timeless works that remain as sharply relevant today as when they were first composed. I have always kept two Shakespearean quotes in the binder of my notepad that I carry to work everyday. One states, "We know what we are, but know not what we may be" (*Hamlet*, Act I, Scene 5), and the other declares, "Our doubts are traitors, and makes us lose the good we oft might win, by fearing to attempt" (*Measure for Measure*, Act I, Scene 4).

16) **_Bill Gates_**. I admire Bill Gates for founding Microsoft and helping to transform the world for the better. Today, many people often want to focus on his philanthropic work, but no matter how many people this worthy action may impact, his business efforts in search for profit far exceed anything the philanthropic work will do. If you disagree, think about how many more philanthropic, business, and medical projects have been developed and operate because of the functionality of Microsoft. These ventures have created wealth, opportunity, and a better quality of life for literally millions of people globally. Such utility surpasses the work Gates has done individually as a philanthropist. Regardless of why one admires him, he followed his dream of developing a system that I am using today to write this very book, and for that, I am so grateful.

17) **_John D. Rockefeller_**. Many people think of John D. Rockefeller for his ruthlessness as a monopolistic business tycoon, but he also had a tremendous positive impact on American society as well. In addition to helping to develop a new industry, he was a man of faith, one who believed God had selected him to make money so he could benefit others. For example, Rockefeller financed considerable medical research and is usually credited with advancements to eradicate hookworm and malaria in the United States. A complex person like many heroes, Rockefeller had purpose, vision, and drive to create value for others. If you wish to know more about this iconic American, I highly recommend the book *Titan* by Ron Chernow.

18) **_Hubert Bond_**. Growing up on the Western Slope of Colorado, I had an old neighbor by the name of Hubert Bond. This man was weathered by the sun and led a challenging life of hard work. My

family was told by other neighbors that Mr. Bond's first wife had been killed when he was plowing the fields with a horse-drawn machine. Though a tough man of the West, Mr. Bond was very kind, with a spirit of peace about him. He taught our family how to irrigate our land with the precious water that was only provided down our ditch every two weeks. He always had time to stop by for a bite to eat and friendly conversation. Though he passed many years ago, I admire Mr. Bond for his strength of will, his unfailing character, and his kindness to others. He was a man who had been hardened by the land and elements, and yet he always took the time to help a neighbor.

19) ***My parents***. Though my parents divorced when I was very young, and my step-father Bill Watson passed away when I was sixteen, I admire all three of them for their love, kindness, and support. Being a parent myself today, I realize how hard it is at times to support a family, to help make ends meet, and to make fair decisions in an ever-changing world. I appreciate that my parents raised me to the best of their ability, and I remain grateful for how they instilled in me a strong work ethic, moral character, a sense of faith, and a love of country. My parents, like yours, were not perfect, but I would not be the person I am today had they not loved me, guided me, and provided me with so many wonderful memories and experiences. I love them to this day, and I hope to be a parent worthy of what they were to me.

20) ***Doug Jackson***. My friend Doug Jackson is the President of Project C.U.R.E., a non-profit organization focused on securing medical supplies for the developing world at no cost. This is

done through receiving donations from the medical community and corporations, usually items they no longer need. Teams of volunteers sort these products and then they are shipped to needed areas throughout the world. These products literally mean the difference between life and death for the people who are receiving them. I admire Doug because he is a man of passion so clearly committed to serving others in love. This man could run a Fortune 500 Company, but instead he has chosen to run the non-profit that his parents founded. His life's question is one we must all consider: "What are you living your life for?" The answer to this question may lead you to love and serve others, whether in a non-profit, another country, in your place or work, or within your community. It is a powerful question that demands a thoughtful answer. Doug lives out this question by serving and loving others in areas that are often overlooked and underserved.

21) ***Steve Jobs***. Though I am a fan and owner of several Apple products, I admire Steve Jobs not for his technical genius, but rather his tenacity of will. After losing Apple, this man came back into a failing company that no one believed in, and helped to guide it into being one of the most transformational companies in the world. Consider how Apple and its products like the iPhone, iTunes, and iPad continue to connect and improve the world in many ways. Jobs had a vision, and he implemented that vision even when others had tried to force him out of it. This took focus, stamina, and strength of will, much needed traits we all must exercise.

22) ***The men and women of the United States Military***. Each time I meet someone serving or who has served in the United States Military, I humbly offer a sincere "thank you" for your service. I

am truly grateful for anyone who has put on a uniform and risked their lives so that the rest of us can enjoy freedom and opportunity. As you know by now, I have traveled to many countries in the world. Although I enjoy visiting them, and appreciate different cultures for various reasons, none compares to our United States of America. Sadly, in many parts of the world others want to destroy and tear down, either because they want to control or to gain power and wealth. We must have individuals who are willing to fight and defend our way of life, to promote liberty, and to protect those who cannot protect themselves. These people put their lives at risk for us, and for that, I am always grateful to them. We should honor them on Memorial Day and Veterans Day, but we should remember and appreciate them every day of the year.

23) ***Mahatma Gandhi***. Gandhi practiced the art of nonviolent civil disobedience. Through this radical method of sacrificing oneself in starvation, imprisonment, and torture, he helped to lead India to its national independence. In this process, he sought to practice truth in all situations, which was not an easy task then, nor is it today. Gandhi was a true servant leader, one who sacrificed himself for the betterment of his fellow people. This is not only admirable, but it was extremely effective in galvanizing his people and the world to his cause of justice and freedom.

24) ***Margaret Thatcher***. This woman was considered the Iron Lady of England. Though she came from modest means, she rose to power at a time when her country was in desperate times with high unemployment and a lack of positive future prospects. Thatcher fought hard to reform her country's government, and she used her wit, charm, and strength of will to change the

course of Great Britain so that its citizens might increase in both financial prosperity and human dignity.

25) ***Don and Gary Stephens***. While visiting my home, the acting Vice President of the United States learned I was from Olathe, Colorado, and asked me if I knew Don and Gary Stephens. Although they're from the same small agricultural ranching community on the western slope of Colorado where I grew up, I didn't know them. It wasn't long, however, until I met them and began serving on their Board of Directors. These brothers helped to found a non-profit many years ago, and now they operate a floating hospital ship that provides free medical care and surgeries to people on the west coast of Africa. These men came from my small town, and now positively impact over 60,000 people per year, not to mention those who serve on board and their accompanying family members.

Once again, this list is by no means exhaustive. As you can see, I tend to admire people who dream big, serve others, love deeply, and try to impact others in some positive transformative way. It is almost always easier to tear down than to build-up. The latter requires strength, time, and force of will, always at some level of personal sacrifice.

Such a price challenges you to ask, "Is what I'm doing truly worth it?" If your answer is "yes," then you must follow your heart, and dare greatly to make the positive impact you wish to see in the world. Whether you succeed or fail, at least you tried, and for this, there is no failure. The only true failure in life is never to try, never to love, never to risk making a positive difference.

RING OF TRUTH
7 QUOTATIONS TO CONSIDER

"Heroes are made by the paths they choose, not the powers they are graced with." | **Brodi Ashton**

"Our heroes are men who do things which we recognize, with regret, and sometimes with a secret shame, that we cannot do. We find not much in ourselves to admire, and we are always privately wanting to be like somebody else. If everybody was satisfied with himself, there would be no heroes." | **Mark Twain**

"Heroes may not be braver than anyone else. They're just braver five minutes longer." | **Ronald Reagan**

"As you get older it is harder to have heroes, but it is sort of necessary." | **Ernest Hemingway**

"The mind is not a vessel to be filled, but a fire to be kindled." | **Plutarch**

"There is nothing I like better than conversing with aged men. For I regard them as travelers who have gone a journey which I too may have to go, and of whom I ought to inquire whether the way is smooth and easy or rugged and difficult. Is life harder toward the end, or what report do you give it?" | **Plato**

"The greatest good you can do for another is not just to share your riches but to reveal to him his own." | **Benjamin Disraeli**

RING OF HONOR

QUESTIONS FOR REFLECTION

Presently, who are your heroes and mentors? Update your list if you have one; if you don't already have a list of heroes and mentors, create one that includes their names and what you specifically admire about them.

_____

_____

_____

_____

_____

What are some of the biggest lessons you have learned from a hero or mentor in your life? How have these lessons inspired you to make certain choices in your life?

_____

_____

_____

_____

_____

Have you ever considered being a mentor to someone else? Though none of us are perfect, we all have something positive to contribute to others.

_____

_____

_____

_____

_____

Do you think that Americans have lost confidence in the idea of having personal heroes? If so, what has caused this loss? What is necessary to restore our faith in public heroes?

_____

_____

_____

_____

_____

If you could change one quality about yourself, what would that be? Would you add a positive trait or instead choose to eliminate what you consider to be a personal weakness or flaw? What lessons can you learn from your heroes or mentors to help you make such a change?

_____

_____

_____

_____

_____

YOUR 7 RINGS:
JOINED AT THE HEART

"The price of greatness is responsibility." | **Winston Churchill**

Many years ago, I decided to be an architect of my life, someone who would be more proactive in my planning and approach, instead of merely reacting to each event that happened to me. This was not easy to do, as it took time and thought, but it has helped make a world of difference. If you seek the same kind of positive influence on your life, then I recommend that you complete the exercises at the end of each chapter of this book, if you have not done so already.

Upon completing these, consider keeping a journal for your ongoing goals and new ideas. Personally, I have kept journals since I was in high school. Though I do not journal every day, I do explore my thoughts in a bound journal from time to time, especially when I read a great quote, hear a good speech or sermon, see a breathtaking panorama in nature, or listen to beautiful music. Keeping a journal has allowed me to keep the 7 Rings before me at all times.

YOUR NEXT SEASON

Sometimes starting a new journal can help reinforce a fresh start and a new season in your life. When I started Northstar Commercial Partners, I bought a leather bound journal with a picture of an old fashioned compass on the cover. I chose this one because I was about to embark upon a journey that could go in many directions, one that needed guidance, that would be worth committing to paper. At the beginning of this particular journal, I wrote down my life's ambitions, goals, and aspirations for my legacy. I then wrote what I wanted to create in a company, how I wanted to impact people positively.

As I've traversed through life, I have also written about the "big events" in my journals. Looking back from time to time, I find it is very helpful to read those old entries, as it gives me perspective on what truly matters, and how many of life's "issues and challenges" are temporary. These entries also help me to remember the abundance of my blessings and the many gifts of a rich and blessed life. As I get older and time takes its toll on my memory and faculties, I know these will only increase in value.

Each January 1, I write down my goals for the New Year. These may range from goals about health, to family, to relationships, to community, and to my business. In other words, they are all goals that revolve in and around my 7 Rings of Life. Throughout the year, at least once a month, I re-read these goals to keep them in mind and also to reflect upon whether they have been met or are still valid. The estimates vary, but most research shows that a person is about 75% more likely to achieve your goals if you write them down and review them. It can never hurt to review your life's goals if they are truly important to you.

I encourage you to prioritize what is important in your life and to consider growing in your love and service to others. We are all busy and the demands of the urgent will consume your time and energy each day, but consider taking the time to go through this exercise carefully and deliberately. Being proactive rather than reactive in laying out the foundation for these priorities will save you tremendous time and stress, and also rescue you from a life of uncertainty. No one wants to miss fulfilling their potential because they constantly lived a reactive life by default.

If you have not done so already, consider keeping a journal about your life. As stated earlier in this book, you are unique, you are special, and you have a story to share. If you have certain aspirations, or want to achieve specific goals, write these down at the beginning of the journal, and explore what is truly important to you, and what you want your life to be.

You are already writing your own life story, and journaling will help you to be an architect and student of your own epic instead of allowing years to pass by without any record, guidance, or accountability. As Socrates pointed out, "The unexamined life is not worth living." You have a unique, one-of-a-kind story to share, and it is one that you can also grow from by writing it down, and occasionally reading it to remind you what is important and how you have grown.

FOCUS AND FILTER

One of the many benefits of my keeping a journal is organization. For instance, I operate the 7 Rings in the context of three primary buckets. The first is my business bucket, where Northstar Commercial Partners and my other business interests reside. The second is philanthropy, where my foundation, my work with the Opportunity Coalition, and other community initiatives operate. The third contains my endeavors in politics and in service to my community, where I try to make a positive impact for my neighbors, team members, colleagues, and fellow citizens.

Cross-pollination occurs among all three of these buckets, but they all rest firmly on the foundation of faith. Many people tend to think of themselves as being only a "business person" or only a "philanthropist." Others may identify with being a "good neighbor" but not a "community activist." For example, I can't tell you how many times my fellow business owners have told me that they "don't get involved in politics," even though politics directly impacts them, positively or negatively, whether they want it to or not.

Each of us is much more complex and dynamic than playing just one role. We may be in business, but we are affected by politics whether we want to be or not. We may think that our philanthropy is outside of the reach of business or politics, but each has their impact on our service initiatives. Each of the three buckets impacts me, and the world I am trying to operate in daily. Whenever possible, I try to determine ways that can benefit each bucket, and help create positive change and impacts for the people I come into contact with.

Although I may have a lot of things going on in my life, distilling everything down to three buckets on the foundation of faith, with the 7 Rings for prioritization, helps create instant and constant clarity for me. I don't have to stop and consider the pros and cons of every daily decision because I can immediately consider them through my existing personal filter.

I encourage you to develop a structure and filter for your life, as it may help you to be more effective, more intentional, and more successful. Try to keep them simple, so you can always remember them, and thereby always act upon them and benefit from them. They will help you focus and filter, preventing you from making poor decisions because of the stress of challenging circumstances.

The more we can focus on maximizing our gifts and fulfilling our divine purpose in life, on how to create benefit for others, then we will in turn live a fulfilled life, both spiritually and financially. "Do well, by doing good" and many great opportunities will present themselves to you. When you use the 7 Rings as your compass, you increase both the joy along your journey as well as the delight of reaching your destination.

IN THE ARENA

As we conclude our journey together within these pages, I hope you have enjoyed this book, and that something I have written has impacted you in some positive way. Let me say once again that I do not have all the answers, as I too am on this journey of learning in life. In this process, I have come to understand a few things in a deeper way, and I have been blessed beyond measure with good health, rich meaningful relationships, love, and the opportunity to impact others for the better.

These 7 Rings are tools I have developed in this journey, and they are by no means all encompassing, or the ones that may work best for you. These are simply the 7 Rings that have had an impact on me, and that act as guideposts for my life. Though they may change in time, they have recurred again and again in my life, to the point that I felt compelled to share them with you.

As with most things in life, there is not one correct formula for success. That being stated, if you are not organized and proactive, you will by nature be unorganized and reactive. Be an architect of your life, vs. someone who has life happen to them. This is within your grasp, and by taking action, you can live a life of positive transformation. The world needs you.

We all know that life can be challenging at times. Please remember that you just may be that inspiration, kindness, or good deed that someone has been hoping for their whole life. Now is your time to act, as you may not be given another opportunity. I learned the importance of this, with the passing of my stepfather. Your call to action may come in the simplest of forms, or more involved projects that can impact thousands and millions of people for the better. It may come from your work in business, philanthropy, politics, or some other area. Regardless of where it comes from, be open for the calling, and receptive to taking action.

When I first started Northstar Commercial Partners many years ago, my wife Patricia gave me one of my all-time favorite quotations beautifully framed, which still rests on a windowsill beside my desk. Taken from a speech by President Theodore Roosevelt, this passage is one I had shared with her many years earlier, and it describes how I view the battlefields that life can bring to us:

> *"It is not the critic who counts; not the man who points out how the strong man stumbles, or where the doer of deeds could have done them better. The credit belongs to the man who is actually in the arena, whose face is marred by dust and sweat and blood; who strives valiantly; who errs, who comes short again and again, because there is no effort without error and shortcoming; but who does actually strive to do the deeds; who knows great enthusiasms, the great devotions; who spends himself in a worthy cause; who at the best knows in the end the triumph of high achievement, and who at the worst, if he fails, at least fails while daring greatly, so that his place shall never be with those cold and timid souls who neither know victory nor defeat."*

I look forward to seeing you out on the arena floor, daring greatly alongside me, as we join together to fight the good battles that matter most! Whether we know victory or defeat, at least we will try to make a positive impact in this life, and be with each other in the one to come. Godspeed on your journey, my friend!

ABOUT THE
AUTHOR

Learn more about Brian Watson at BrianWatson.us.

COMMON THREADS
QUOTES AND SAYINGS

1. _____

2. _____

3. _____

4. _____

5. _____

6. _____

7. _____

8. _____

9. _____

10. _____

11. _____

12. _____

13. _____

14. _____

15. _____

16. _____

17. _____

18. _____

19. _____

20. _____

21. _____

22. _____

23. _____

24. _____

25. _____

26. _____

27. _____

28. _____

29. _____

30. _____

31. _____

32. _____

33. _____

34. _____

35. _____

36. _____

37. _____

38. _____

39. _____

40. _____

41. _____

42. _____

43. _____

44. _____

45. _____

46. _____

47. _____

48. _____

49. _____

50. _____

NOTES

NOTES